T0333457

ELIZABETH CHOY

Cover: Detail of a portrait taken by a
London society photographer in 1953 when
Elizabeth Choy represented Singapore at the
Coronation of Queen Elizabeth II.

LANDMARK BOOKS PTE LTD
106, Clementi St 12
#04-44 Singapore 120106
Landmark Books is an imprint
of Landmark Books Pte Ltd

ISBN 978-981-18-6492-6

Printed in Singapore

ELIZABETH CHOY

A War Heroine and More

A Biography by Zhou Mei

·LANDM△RK·BOOKS·

Thanks are due to

Mrs Elizabeth Choy Su-Moi
for her invaluable co-operation, without which
this book would not have seen print.

FOREWORD

CARING, ALTRUISTIC AND STEADFAST: these were the qualities that Mummy embodied as a war heroine and throughout her life.

Growing up, we knew Mummy was a special lady even before we fully understood what 'war heroine' meant. She was highly respected by everyone, and many were drawn to her – especially as she grew older. The doors of our home were open to people from all walks of life: from the blind or anyone in need, to doctors, philanthropists, and university lecturers. As Mummy often said, she was just as comfortable dining with the Queen (which she did) as she would with a pauper. Never one to discriminate, she treated all with respect, with an extra portion of compassion for the poor and handicapped.

Mummy showed her care in little ways. She was a good listener and gave good advice so, unfailingly, we would come away from talking to her feeling lightened. We will never forget what she once said: "Unless you can think of something good to say about a person, it is better not to say anything. And when you do speak, give an encouraging word if it is helpful; even a smile and greeting to a cleaner can help to bring some cheer to another dreary day for them." Without saying much, Mummy provided comfort to many who sought her counsel or just sheer, pleasant company. Irene remembers studying into the wee hours of the morning in the dining room, wordlessly accompanied by Mummy, who would read the Bible or practice her Jawi in the kitchen. It was her way of saying you were not alone while everyone was in bed.

Always compassionate with a magnanimous love for others, Mummy would put the needs of others before her own, even strangers. She opened our home to those in need and sought temporary shelter. Strangers, friends and relatives were welcomed warmly and were all treated with the same care and compassion, regardless of ethnicity or abilities. Ever altruistic, she could not say "no" when approached for help, even from people she hardly knew and when helping required sacrifice on her part. One night in the early 1960s, a man who had been scalded by a spilt pot of boiling hot oil while cooking in a coffee shop was brought to Mummy instead of the hospital – perhaps she was seen as someone to go to when in dire need. She put others first even when she was hospitalised for the last time.

Mummy's strength – physically, emotionally and spiritually – was indisputably her greatest attribute that we especially admire. At the age of 57, she hopped agilely from rock to rock on the promontory of Pulau Pangkor and duckwalked her way through the Göreme caves in Turkey when she was 82. Mummy possessed great determination. When she had a stroke in her early 90s and was transferred to a community hospital for physiotherapy treatment, her determination enabled her to recover faster than others who were younger than she was. Her resolve to recover continued at home as she practised daily on the stairs till she was able to walk without aid, though more slowly and with a guiding arm when she went out. Mummy's unwavering faith in God gave her the strength to withstand the torture she experienced during World War II. She was so strong even though she was terribly malnourished! Mummy would recount how, during the war, she cleaned the only commode in the *Kempeitai* cell shared by all, including many who were suffering from dysentery. This she did with a little rag and a small stone to scrape away the dirt.

Beyond her title of War Heroine, Mummy was a doting and devoted mother. She drove us to and fro for all our piano lessons and math tuition. She never shouted at us if we did anything wrong, but instead patiently explained to us why and what we did was not right. Mummy also made an effort to connect with our fads and interests, from buying us the latest tent dresses to listening to us rattle on about popular music and shows. Lynette recalls the time Mummy accompanied us – dressed smartly in her cheongsam – to the hotel in the old Cathay building to try to get the autographs of the actors of *The Man from U.N.C.L.E.* television series when it was rumoured they were staying there. (We returned home rather crestfallen without an autograph.) Without fail, she made sure we felt loved and supported constantly, often through small actions like giving us warm, tight hugs whenever she was pleased with us or to encourage us. Irene will never forget what Mummy once said to her when she told Mummy not to worry about her: "I will always worry about you until I close my eyes forever."

In the extended family, Mummy was a wonderful mother-in-law, doting grandmother and the best sister-in-law; a living saint in *gu-ma*'s words. Irene's husband, Michael, enjoyed her company so much so that once in Bangkok, he gave Irene extra cash to go shopping with the children so that he could spend more time in a small café to watch the world go by with Mummy. She showed the same dedication to her grandchildren, for instance, patiently going through school or tuition work with Stefanie, Bridget's daughter, on a daily basis and even learning Chinese so that she could teach her. She had an excellent relationship of warmth, respect and affection with her own family and Daddy's. She kept close contact with her Yong relatives throughout her life, especially her only brother and his wife. In her old age, Mummy met different groups on a regular or weekly basis, going to their homes or to favourite haunts to have meals together. Our uncle told Bridget that Mummy sent him a letter thanking him for "another enjoyable day" after every outing.

Her generosity and kindness won the love and respect of the Choy extended family as well. We came to know some of our Choy cousins when Mummy hosted Daddy's eldest brother's family for a couple of years while their house was being built.

All through her life, Mummy loved parties and meeting people. She built friendships and brought people together to bond family ties. She intentionally put into practice the beatitude "Blessed are the peacemakers, for they shall be called the children of God." Despite all the terrible experiences she had gone through, Mummy learnt to forgive and forget, a virtue hard to achieve for many. She told Cheryl, Irene's daughter, when she did her History project on the Japanese Occupation in school: "Don't blame/dislike the person(s). Hate the circumstances they found themselves in that resulted in their actions."

Lynette's daughter, Andrea, put this well: "*Por Por* has held many important titles like war heroine, politician, principal and teacher, and garnered many prestigious awards. However, these have little meaning unless you knew the person she was. She was strong, gentle, always loving and ever giving, full of integrity and cloaked with grace; a genuine gem in character and a role model in how she lived her Christian faith. Everyone in the family agrees that it was truly a privilege to have known her and to have been loved by her. While she fully deserved the accolades she received in her lifetime she remains to us our sweet, cherished, and beloved mummy and *Por Por*."

Colin, Irene's son, adds, "I have not experienced or observed anyone make such an impact on people the way my grandmother had, and perhaps still does today. Respectful, gracious, resilient, humble, helpful, forgiving – these are among the so many words you could use to describe her. In just as many ways you could learn to live your life from her. She was positive and put most importance in treating others well. She was not one to fuss, and was modest of her achievements. I experienced the legacy of her character and humility during my school days. She was an ex-VP of St Andrew's Junior School and teachers who knew I was her grandson would sometimes ask how she was. Even canteen staff remembered her."

Mummy's life was filled with ups and downs, yet she never once faltered. She lived her values and beliefs in every step, many of which we strive to emulate. We learnt to be kind, patient and compassionate to the less fortunate and others, accepting people from different backgrounds as they are with respect. She showed Christian love and care.

Her spiritual steadfastness taught us to have an inner strength and God's peace that comes from trusting the Lord Jesus and going to him in prayer; to always do our best and leave the rest to God. She was a truly courageous, compassionate and altruistic person throughout her well-lived life of 96 years. We feel so privileged to have shared a part of it.

Bridget, Lynette and Irene Choy

CONTENTS

PROLOGUE

NUMBER ONE Orchard Road. An innocuous address. But to Singaporeans, for whom the number one is to be treasured, it is a prestigious one, drawing attention and commanding premium. And on Orchard Road at that. The street's fame as the shopping belt of the Republic is renowned well beyond the shores of this island. It has, of course, been transformed beyond recognition over the decades, from a road lined with rows of double-storey shophouses and showrooms to one defined by gleaming skyscrapers. Those familiar with the locale would know that to the building's right, separated by Fort Canning Road, is the National Museum. On its left, a Presbyterian Church founded in 1878. Across the street, the Cathay Building, the original completed in 1941; Singapore's tallest edifice when the island-colony fell to the Japanese in 1942.

To Elizabeth Choy Su-Moi, however, One Orchard Road was the fount of unspeakable evil, the nightmare she wished to forget, but couldn't. For years, she went out of her way to avoid it; she would rather waste time getting to her destination via a circuitous route than be in its vicinity. For it was to this address that the newly-wed Elizabeth was taken one calamitous day, 15 November 1943, by the Japanese Military Police, the *Kempeitai*. It was here that the

Japanese incarcerated, abused and tortured her; here that she was confronted with incomprehensible cruelty and brutality at the hands of her fellowmen; here that she experienced hell on earth; here that she was sentenced to death by decapitation.

A half century after, Elizabeth Choy Su-Moi had resolutely put aside her nightmare by focusing on the joy of being among the living. Her regular appearance at One Orchard Road was not only testimony to her resolve but also to the promise she made herself to extend her hand to those in need, no matter who they are. It was a strange and poignant sight to behold: this ramrod-straight octogenarian keeping pace alongside the multiple-handicapped, muscularly-built Maria Theresa Chan Poh Lin, born in the year the Japanese surrendered. Without fail, on alternate Wednesday mornings, the one served as the eyes and ears of the other. Their destination: Number One Orchard Road.

I

BORN FREE

YONG SU-MOI was born in 1910, the Year of the Dog, in a little settlement called Kudat, towards the northern tip of British North Borneo – the Land Below the Wind. The region had come under British control in the late nineteenth century. In 1872, the Sultan of Sulu gave William Cowie, a gun-runner, the right to establish a base at Sandakan Bay. Later, control of much of North Borneo passed into the hands of the Dent brothers, Alfred and Edward. They formed a limited provisional association which, by 1882, had evolved into the British North Borneo Company, incorporated by royal charter. In 1888, the territory became a British protectorate. Today it is known as Sabah and has been, since 1963, a state of Malaysia.[1]

Su-Moi's ancestors were of Hakka stock, the only dialect group without a territorial base of its own; the people were originally inhabitants of northern China. Some time in history, they were forced to flee southwards where most of them settled in the provinces of Guangdong and Fujian. But they did not assimilate well, remaining distinctive, clinging on to their dialect and its several sub-varieties. The fact that they did not quite belong wherever they might have settled is lucidly reflected in the name Hakka, literally meaning 'guests', underscoring their transience. To this day, the Hakkas are proud of their own resilience to hardship. They contend that it is their inner strength, reinforced by their sturdy physique, that has made it possible for them to have withstood hostility at the hands of their fellow beings. Material deprivation, it seems, merely toughened them.

It was some time in the latter part of the nineteenth century when the Yongs embraced Christianity. It is possible that members of the family first worked for German missionaries in China. Or Su-Moi's great-grandparents could have moved to Hongkong – the Fragrant Harbour ceded to the British under the Treaty of Nanjing of 1842 – in response to employment opportunities offered by the missionaries based there. Whichever the case, it is on record that there was an offer made in Hongkong in the early 1880s, directed at the Hakkas, of free passage to British North Borneo, a sparsely populated land in need of settlers. In response, a small reconnaissance group, led by a priest, set out to investigate the offer in that vast unknown. Negotiations with the Governor, W. H. Treacher, came to fruition in April 1883 with the arrival of the first Hakka Christian community, a group of ninety-six, pioneers all.[2]

Su-Moi's grandparents were probably among them. They were undaunted by the all-encompassing jungle. Coming from overpopulated China, they, the landless of their motherland, were eager to till the virgin soil. Indeed, it was the prospect of having a plot to cultivate and call their own that enticed them to leave the familiarity of home for the unknown. In that vast, primitive land, the native Kadazans far outnumbered the handful of ethnic Chinese who had come to settle in the lush tropics. But there was land aplenty for anyone who cared to toil. It was back-breaking work transforming the dense jungle into orderly plantations. Every chore had to be manually done. First, the trees had to go, via the slash-and-burn method of cultivation – the only one known to the settlers. The trunks were left to dry and rot where they fell. When sufficiently dried, it would be bonfire time, which could go on for several days. After the fires had died and the ground was cool again, it would finally be time to plant. By then, the soil would be fertile and ready to reward those who tilled it. Progress was painfully slow but the settlers were determined. Like the other pioneers, the Yongs first started with a single hectare; then another; then a few more; in time, it would expand to several hundreds. Coconut trees – the 'trees of life' – sprouted. Next came rubber; then pepper and coffee as well. The Yongs were devout Christians, who not only passed on their faith to the younger generations but also took care of the spiritual needs of the community. Kudat was divided into several settlements and Su-Moi's paternal grandfather, Yong Sinn-Siong, was in charge of what was known as the 'old settlement'. He preached every Sunday to his fellow Chinese Christians and was responsible for the welfare of all Christians there. In addition, he was also the schoolmaster, the one and only in that settlement. Su-Moi's maternal grandfather, Wong Tien-Nyuk, was the priest in charge of the whole of Kudat town. He was thus responsible for all the settlements of Kudat, including that under the charge of Yong Sinn-Siong.

Clearly, being Christian did not mean giving up their ethnicity or their ancestry. Despite having settled in their host country, China was still *the* homeland to the pioneers. To ensure that his sons kept their Chinese roots, Yong Sinn-Siong carried on the practice of many overseas Chinese: he sent them back to China to not only study the language, but also live with his fellow countrymen and, in this manner, be immersed in the culture for a few years at least. Thus, when the time was ripe, the eldest of the eleven children (five boys and six girls), Su-Moi's father, set sail for China with a younger brother. By the time the boys returned to North Borneo, their Chineseness would be erosion-proof.

Yong Thau-Yin returned to North Borneo and went on to complete his education in the English medium. In those days, mission schools – Anglican, Lutheran, Roman Catholic – were the only ones in North Borneo. Since the area around Kudat came under the German mission, Su-Moi's father finished his schooling in a Lutheran-run school. The English literacy he acquired secured him a government post, to work as a civil servant. He married Wong Pui Chin, the daughter of Wong Tien-Nyuk, in Kudat in 1909. They were to have six children with Su-Moi as the first-born. The family seemed to be constantly on the move as his job required him to serve in different districts of North Borneo. Before long, they were off to Jesselton. Then it was Keningau.

Su-Moi's earliest memories are of the little township of Keningau, deep in the interior. Her nanny, a Kadazan, had the badly stained teeth of most Kadazans, probably the result of tobacco and areca-nut chewing; it was from her that the infant Su-Moi learned to utter her first language – Kadazan. The nanny would take her charge to the river-bank within sauntering distance from her parents' house in the clearing. This was the natural venue for friends to gather, not only to update each other with the latest goings-on, but also to do their laundry and their own ablutions. It was a marvellous playground and a rich store of shiny beads – probably pebbles – which the toddler found mesmerising.

She was blissfully ignorant of racial distinctions and religious differences. Though born to devout Christians, the pagans were nevertheless her people. The Kadazans were warm and loving. Many a time she watched wide-eyed and awed as they worshipped. The rituals were simple, yet impressive and moving even to a child. The Yongs' wooden house was on a hillock, at the foot of which was an outcrop of gigantic rocks. From the crevices, clumps of papaya trees sprouted, flowered and fruited. The natives would gather at one of the rocks, chosen to serve as an altar, an altar created and moulded by mother nature. On this, they would solemnly place offerings of eggs, fruit, flowers, tobacco and rice – or whatever other produce they had – and prostrate themselves before it in homage to their maker.

Equally fascinating were those big jars and very roughly-hewn structures with heads – yes, these once belonged to humans – hanging from their rafters. The heads were proof of valour, mostly collected by the headman and other valiant men of the district. The native chief took great pride in showing off his collection to visitors.

They were right there in the state-room, a structure of four posts, four beams and a roof. Here too would be the gongs, the earthen vessels, ceremonial jars and pots.

Newly-severed heads were a familiar sight to Su-Moi. As the sun cast a mellow glow in its retreat for the day, Su-Moi would often be found sitting on the wooden steps of their home, flanked by a younger brother and sister. The older girl would have her arms protectively round the two siblings and three pairs of curious eyes would watch the world go by. Coming into view, the evening procession of Kadazans, back from yet another day of hunting and score-settling, would walk erectly and regally by, carrying colourful long spears and blowpipes over their lean and muscular shoulders. Their 'trophies' of the day would be very visible, dangling and swaying to the rhythm of the victors' gait. But the hunters seemed quite harmless to the children; they saw nothing intimidating in them nor were they frightened at the sight of the day's harvest, be it jungle fowl, wild boar or human head. Fear was an emotion alien to Su-Moi and her siblings.

To the young Su-Moi, beheading seemed within the natural order of things. Horror and revulsion would come only when she became educated and sophisticated in urbanised Singapore. To one born in the wild, it was merely the way of the people. If there were any police or courts, these would be too far away to intervene or arbitrate when differences arose among the people. As she understood it, if a tribe learnt that it was the target of another's evil intent, surely it was only right for it to retaliate. Or, if the misdeed was actually committed, then surely it was only right to go after the perpetrators and mete out the only punishment known to the tribes: decapitation. The public display of the severed heads would serve as an effective warning to others who might be harbouring similar intent. The bravery of the man who succeeded in beheading his enemies, moreover, would be shared by his whole tribe. So the heads were to his credit as well as to his tribe's. Su-Moi saw nothing wrong in such thinking. Her Christian parents and their parents before them accepted the ways of the people. To condemn was not their way. An unstated rule in that community was respect for others' ways, culture and religion.

This mutual respect extended as well to the sprinkling of Malays in the largely Chinese settlement. The first encounter Su-Moi had with Muslim practices involved the slaughter of a cow. One day, there was the need to butcher a cow but Su-Moi overheard the grown-ups saying that they had to wait for the *Tuan Haji*. With the curiosity of a child, she tagged along to see for herself what a *Tuan Haji* was.[3] That was when she discovered that the person was a Malay man who would say a prayer before the cow was killed. Total enlightenment as to why it had to be so had to wait somewhat longer, when she studied Malay literature, but for the child, the incident impressed upon her proper respect for the ways of others.

Su-Moi was still a pre-schooler when her father's job as a district officer took him to another part of the country: Tenom. It was hardly a town – it did not even have a marketplace, nor any stores selling garments or footwear; there were just a few provision shops offering a very limited range of goods: some dried foodstuff and pots and pans. Yet, in comparison to Keningau, Tenom, the terminus of the railway from Jesselton (now Kota Kinabalu), was rated as far more developed and civilised. However, there were no schools in Tenom. When it was time for her to begin her formal education, Su-Moi was enrolled in the school in Kudat run by her paternal grandfather and would have to live with her grandparents. Getting there from Tenom took some planning and time. She had to go to Jesselton by rail, then cross over to Kudat by boat. That wasn't journey's end. After the boat trip came a buffalo-cart ride on a road – barely a mud track – which was invariably in a very bad state. The ride would be at a snail's pace. Then it was 'home': a rather crudely put together structure worthy of its pioneer status.

To an adult, it would have been a terribly tedious journey. To a child, however, it was pure adventure. For Su-Moi, the train journey was most fascinating and memorable. The very thought of that journey makes her nostalgic for the wonderful carefree days. She took her first train ride to Jesselton when she was about seven years old. To this day, she can vividly visualise it. The panoramic scenery unfolding before her as she perched on the hard seat of the train, eyes transfixed, as it chortled on its track. A breath-taking gorge with rushing torrents and steep banks lay on one side of the railroad; marvelous animals flashed past, some grazing contentedly, others exuding the joy of living as they galloped freely in the verdant land; gorgeously plumed birds, large and small, exhibitionists all, flapped and flew before her eyes. There was so much to see; certainly far too many species for the child to try to identify or count.

In Kudat, the little schoolhouse was less than a kilometre away from Su-Moi's grandparents' home. It was thus not at all difficult to get to school on foot, using a footpath. The school-house was a single large room. The schoolmaster – Grandfather Yong himself – was in sole charge of all the children, totalling perhaps a few scores of young boys and girls. The children would be seated at crudely-made desks, with the younger or smaller ones nearer to the front where there was a larger desk and a chair for the schoolmaster. Behind this hung a blackboard on the wall. Lessons would involve recitation in which every child participated, parrot-like. There would also be some written work. Grandfather Yong taught in his own dialect, Hakka. Most of the children were from Hakka families; however, the few who were not did not seem to have any difficulty following the lessons. No one misbehaved either. The children knew better than to cross a schoolmaster who knew all their parents and, to boot, would also be the preacher come Sunday.

Later, when her brother Kon Vui needed to attend school, he had a far more daunting journey before him. Kon Vui and an uncle of about his age would have to make an early start as their school was some six kilometres away. To get there, they trekked along narrow footpaths through thick undergrowth and tall, sharp-edged *lalang*. It would be the time of the morning when all vegetation would be laden with dew; and those who ventured out were resigned to arriving at their destination quite damp. Then there were not only mosquitoes but scorpions, centipedes and leeches too, awful blood-sucking creatures. The leeches were definitely the worst. However, everyone knew how to get rid of those tenacious creatures: wood ash would do the trick; salt would be just as effective; if you could not lay your hands on these, then try your own spittle. It was just humanly impossible to keep a safe distance from the leeches, on land or in water. Over the years, however, the boys' mode of transportation would improve tremendously: first they would go to school on horseback, then came bicycles.

On Saturdays and Sundays, when there was no school, Su-Moi would accompany her elders on their plantation supervision rounds. The Chinese were notoriously disdainful of being employed; everyone wanted to be his own boss. Far better to be your own man, even if what you could call yours was just a tiny plot of land. In any case, there were far too few Chinese around to be employed as labourers. The plantation workers were mostly Kadazans. They knew instinctively when to come; for instance, in time to pluck the coconuts. Men and women would troop in in the hundreds, almost on cue, to help harvest the crop. They would stay till the work was done, usually about two to three weeks.

In another setting, the attire of the Kadazans – or lack of it – would probably have raised not a few prudish brows. For the men, a belt round the waist and a piece of bark between the legs completed their outfits. For the bare-breasted women: a tiny mini skirt. Some of the women would be bedecked with necklaces of the shiny greyish beads found on river banks and gleaming brass bangles worn in a spiral round their arms and legs. Everyone would have flowers – wild orchids – in their jet-black hair. On festive occasions, they would wear special belts, some made of coins linked together. It was the fashion to wear several belts at the same time, forming a sort of a corset round the wearers' bellies and, as they walked, the ornaments made enchanting music. Su-Moi found all of them attractive and graceful. To the wideeyed girl, all before her was absolutely gorgeous and stunning.

The Kadazans were paid on a piece-rate basis. If the plantation owner – in this case, Grandfather Yong – wanted to clear the undergrowth around the coconut trees, each worker would be paid according to the number of trees around which he or she had cleared. But the Kadazans had yet to learn how to count. The simple solution to their innumeracy was in knots. They cleverly twisted bark into string and after attending to the work around a tree, tied one knot on the string. At the end of the day, each worker would bring his or her string to Grandfather Yong and the accounts could be done very quickly by counting the number of knots. Of course, implicit mutual trust was involved in this system.

The observant Su-Moi noticed that when any Kadazan was given something to take home, her grandfather would always write his name as well as that of the Kadazan on the parcel. He explained that this would prevent misunderstanding as the Kadazans would have to trek through other settlers' plantations before reaching home. He did not want his workers to be accused of stealing.

The Yong children were taught from a young age that all work is noble. Each of them helped in the plantation, whether it be to plant coconuts, hook the nuts from the trees or split them to get at the kernels which would then be dried in the sun. They did their share of work alongside the Kadazans, completely at ease with each other. The elder Yongs did not discriminate between the genders, but in the assignment of duties around the homestead, they impressed upon the young ones that there was a distinction between girls and boys. Thus, while everyone worked in the fields, the girls would be required to help with the cooking at home and learn how to sew, while the boys would be given extra chores to do outdoors.

One chore involved the buffaloes. These animals were used for carrying heavy loads, often over considerable distances. Each buffalo had a crudely made saddle which provided a seat for the buffalo-herd while gunny-sackfuls of goods would be slung over the animal's broad back. After the day's work was done, the children would lead the buffaloes to the river to bathe and relax. (The rule, work before play, applied to both people and animals.) But buffaloes, being buffaloes, would sometimes decide to take a break when work was not quite done. This happened when there was a need to cross streams and brooks. On a hot day, a buffalo would instinctively lie down when there was water under its belly. When it did so, everything on its back would get a soaking. No amount of 'heave-ho's from the children could get the animal to stand up when it was not ready to do so. The children learnt to pre-empt any recurrence. To outsmart the animal, they would get down from the buffalo before reaching any water and lead it across as quickly as possible – before it realised there was water about. If it were just a pool or pond before them, to keep temptation from the animal, the children would skirt it.

Often, there would be a crocodile or two almost submerged in the river, immobile but watchful. The children had been taught not to tease or disturb crocodiles but being children, there were lapses. It was irresistible: there they were, ferocious, mean-looking creatures basking motionless on the banks, casting such sly and defiant glares at the children – sitting targets, really. It was just too tempting. Someone would start by picking up pebbles and throwing them at the crocodiles. Then another child would do likewise; soon, there would be a shower of pebbles raining on the indolent reptiles. Fortunately for the children, the crocodiles did not react – other than the odd one that seemed to wink at the children's antics. They were perhaps too comfortable to stir; or considered the children unworthy foes; or perhaps they had already had their meal for the day. In any case, the crocodiles left the children and the buffaloes under their care be. The buffaloes would be content, lying in the water, quite still except for the slow blinking of their drooping eyelids.

Thumb-sized leeches clung onto the buffaloes when they got out of the water. It was not possible even for the jungle-wise to get used to leeches. Su-Moi for one. When confronted by those crawlies, the sangfroid and equanimity so characteristic of her would take flight. The revulsion for those blood-suckers has remained with her as an adult, and if any living creature could make Su-Moi panic and scream, it is the leech. "They burrow under your skin and suck and suck and suck. Only when they have had enough of your blood, when their bellies balloon, only then would they withdraw and drop to the ground." She shudders at the very thought of ever encountering leeches again.

There was the day, for instance, when she and some young friends on their way to her family's plantation passed a stream and could not resist the water snails in the sparklingly clear water. Water snails, it seems, are much like escargot – nutritious and delicious. Reckoning their mothers would be pleased to have the snails for an additional dinner dish, the girls merrily rolled up their trousers, waded into the water and made a bountiful harvest; their baskets were soon brimful with snails. Their glee was short lived, however, for as they smugly clambered out of the stream, one girl spotted a leech on another's leg; then another on another's, till it became apparent that every leg was covered with leeches! Mass hysteria reigned as the girls screeched in fright and panic.

Living in the wild as Su-Moi did, there was just no way she could avoid those awful tenacious leeches, though admittedly, at times, she seemed to be asking for it. For instance, she could not resist dangling her legs in the water when she went to the jetty near her home. She would do so, perhaps to catch up with some reading; or just to cool off and while away a little time between chores. The water was irresistibly cool and soothing; just as her legs in the water were irresistible to the leeches lying in wait.

In other respects as well, nature was bountiful; no one went hungry. There was no need for prepacked lunches or water bottles as there were fruit trees all round: Banana, mango, pomelo and many, many others. They belonged to no one and everyone. Guavas, a favourite, were specially abundant. She and her siblings gorged on these with abandon despite the adults' warning that overeating guavas could trigger appendicitis. In any event, none of their appendixes ever protested. However, they took another warning seriously and obeyed strictly: never drink unboiled water. But they never had to go thirsty. One merely had to scale a coconut tree and pluck a fruit. No one needed a monkey to do that; climbing trees was as natural a locomotive skill as walking to the children. And all of them could wield the *parang*, a curved, cleaver-like knife favoured by the natives. Whack, and the kernel would be split. Of course, if it were the coconut water you wanted, you should just hack away the top, lift the whole nut, tilt and drink.

The children also climbed trees for fun. Often, about a dozen – mostly siblings and uncles and aunts of the same age group – would vie with each other to scale the tallest tree in the fastest time. Su-Moi was never one to turn down a challenge. She relished it. But once, her zest to be champion almost cost her dearly. That was the day when she was alone and decided to do some practising. She went swiftly up the trunk of a coconut tree, then reached up for a frond to give her leverage to heave herself further up. However, carelessly, she had not bothered to look up or she would have noticed that the frond immediately overhead was decayed. Before she could holler, she was down and out on the ground. Fortunately, she survived with nothing worse than some bruises and a temporarily dampened zeal for climbing.

In the jungle, be prepared for the unexpected, even in the climbing of trees and the plucking of fruit. No, you would not be breaking any man-made law, but you might just be infringing the territorial rights of creatures which do not take kindly to human intrusion. Imagine the state of Su-Moi's mind when she happily climbed a tree whose ripe juicy fruit beckoned her, only to spot two glittering eyes staring at her with wishful venom, the reptilian coil tensed to strike. There was no time to apply general knowledge, no time to tell herself that it was but a harmless non-venomous snake. No, it was retreat first and reason later.

Snakes of course were very much part of jungle life. The children learnt early to tell the harmless from the poisonous. Most of the snakes they came across were non-venomous but there were nevertheless dangerous ones of either category lurking around, often in the most unlikely places. Once, one of Su-Moi's aunts needed one of the baskets hanging from the eaves outside Grandfather Yong's house. Su-Moi helped her to bring one down, using a long pole with a hook at the end. They were surprised by its weight and soon found out why. Coiled cosily inside was a handsome python, fast asleep, after having helped itself to a satisfying meal of about a dozen eggs from the chicken coop. It was obvious that the python had swallowed the eggs whole; their shapes could be seen – and counted – in its belly.

Survival in the wild was learnt by observation; much of the settlers' knowledge of nature's bounty and survival skills was gleaned from the Kadazans. No Kadazan would be without a *parang*. It was not from any paranoia of ambush by their enemies; it was a basic tool for clearing undergrowth. Of course, it could be a lethal weapon to kill too – for food. Should a fire be needed, there was no need for matches. Just watch the Kadazans. Select the right dry twigs and rub them against each other. It never failed to start a fire. The children also learnt from the Kadazans the fastest way up a tree, the least painful means of getting honey, the best berries to pick, which tubers and roots were edible and which animals to hunt. Meat could be from a monkey, a crocodile, a squirrel, a wild fowl and even a horse. They all tasted equally delicious.

The settlers needed no organised campaigns to encourage them to support one another. In that environ, the spirit and practice of *gotong royong* – mutual self-help – were exemplary and came naturally. Everyone knew everyone else. Religion was doubtless a unifying factor, and the church the focal point of communal activities. (People would turn out in full force every Sunday morning for service at eleven o'clock after which some would go to town with the farm produce while others would be back to work on their plantations.) Just about every family occasion would be shared with the whole community, be it a wedding, a birth or a death. When the occasion called for celebration, the settlement's best cooks would be ready to do their part. When there was an emergency – say a fire – help was summoned by ringing the church bell. People would drop whatever they were doing and come running, ready to help.

There were few occasions in the year when the industrious settlers could relax and enjoy themselves. Needless to say, when such a day came, the children were the ones who did so with utmost gusto. There was Christmas; very special to the settlement of Christians.

To the children, Christmas Eve was the best. There would be a huge Christmas tree, colourfully decorated to enchant the goggling youngsters. There were Christmas goodies: Cakes, sweets and nuts, and, to add to the festive air, make-shift firecrackers, made of pieces of bamboo to produce sharp and loud bursting sounds – not unlike the sound of gunshots.

Equally important was the Lunar New Year. Whatever their religion, the settlers were proud of their ethnicity. Tradition must be upheld and practised, children taught the ways of the ancestors. Preparations would begin about a month before with the momentum picking up as the day drew nearer. New garments were made for all the children; cakes and sweetmeats were cooked and kept safely out of their reach. The New Year's Eve dinner was one of the very rare occasions when a pig would be slaughtered. Before partaking of the feast, the eldest in the family, with family members standing beside him, would say grace.

Festive food was a treat for the settlers whose daily fare was simple: rice and vegetables from their garden plots, supplemented by fish from the rivers. (Every household was, of course, well stocked with salted fish as a standby.) Chicken would only be served when the family had special reason to celebrate. Even eggs were too precious for daily consumption. A child would probably get a hard-boiled egg all to herself or himself only on a birthday or as a special reward for being good or doing well in school.

Su-Moi's seventh birthday was a memorable day. (It was her last before leaving her parents to live with her grandparents in Kudat.) Many people were invited to the occasion: Children and adults, relatives and friends, including many Kadazans. But, no birthday cake or candles; no one sang 'Happy Birthday'. Instead, there was a basket of more than one hundred hard-boiled eggs to celebrate her special day. For drinks, boiled river water, and as dessert, a rich variety of jungle fruit. The main source of fun and entertainment came from a pair of binoculars belonging to Su-Moi's father. Everyone took turns to peer through the 'wonder glasses' at the distant hills; especially excited and thrilled were the Kadazans as they clamoured for their turn. Su-Moi recalled: "I well remember how the Kadazan women laughed and marvelled at the 'magic' instrument."

---

1   The state covers a land area of nearly 80,000 sq km on the huge island of Borneo. To its north are the South China and Sulu seas; to its south-west, the fellow Malaysian state of Sarawak; and to its south, Kalimantan (Indonesian Borneo).

2   Source: *A History of Modern Sabah: 1881-1963* by K G Tregonning (University of Singapore, 1965).

3   A Muslim man who has been to Mecca on pilgrimage would have Haji before his name; Tuan is the polite form of address for such a person.

II

LIFE IN THE WILD

SU-MOI'S FAMILY was, to her, a perfect unit. It was a typical Chinese extended family where the hierarchy was clear-cut. At the apex were her grandparents, the most senior living members. They had authority over the whole family. Next came her parents who were directly in charge of their children's welfare and upbringing. The children were brought up to respect their elders – none would ever dare challenge the authority of the grown-ups. And as was the way with Chinese, a certain distance was maintained between parent and child. Children were always restrained in their behaviour before their parents, but when father and mother were out of sight and hearing – well, that would be something else. It did not, however, mean that Su-Moi and her siblings did not have fun with their father and mother. She well remembers many happy family times together.

The evening meal was followed by vespers. With Su-Moi's mother at the organ, a hymn would be sung by all, most heartily by the children. Grandfather Yong would say a prayer and read the Bible. (Often, this would be followed by the younger members of the family taking turns to read – "like reading lessons, in Hakka, of course." The children were mesmerised by the Bible stories.)

Thus, the values of the elders and Bible teachings were transmitted and, in the process, traditional Chinese family values and Christian obligations assimilated. So it was there in the tropical wild east, under the watchful gaze of her elders that Su-Moi learnt right from wrong. The values inculcated in her during those early years were to remain intact in the years ahead when she left home for studies; the same values would see her through extreme hardship and exasperation in her adult life.

One of Su-Moi's fondest memories was of the time spent with Grandfather Yong in the evenings before bedtime – astronomy time. The large platform in the compound used for drying copra would serve as their observatory. After vespers, her grandfather would tell the children (both grandchildren and the younger of his eleven children) to lie down on the platform and the lesson would begin. He would point out the stars in the mysterious night sky. It never failed to thrill and enthrall the children, to be able to recognise and name those distant constellations. He would also tell stories, mostly from the Bible, as well as folk-tales of the land of his ancestors. When the children fell asleep on the platform, he would not have the heart to wake them up, but would carry them one by one to their beds.

Looking back, Su-Moi realises that her family was quite exceptional. Both sets of grandparents were educated; not just the two grandfathers but the grandmothers too. Her maternal grandfather, Wong Tien-Nyuk, was renowned in the settlement for his erudition. Her paternal grandfather, Yong Sinn-Siong, was the schoolmaster. Both grandfathers were also preachers. Both their families were well known and respected for their social work. No one in need of help was ever turned away. With the seat of government, Sandakan, so far away, settlers with disputes had to devise a more speedy means of getting problems solved among themselves. The practice was to turn to respected members of the community and Grandfather Yong was one of them. Meetings would be held right there at his house and without fail, whatever the problem, it would be resolved to the satisfaction of all concerned.

Typical of her generation, Su-Moi's mother was self-reliant. Among her many roles as mistress of the household was that of family seamstress; all her children were neatly dressed in clothes stitched and embroidered by her. She also tended her vegetable patch which provided for the family table. There was, on the maternal side, a very good organist who played every Sunday in church, and it was probably from him that Su-Moi's mother learnt to play the organ. She was also adept at floral arrangement. Su-Moi remembers her mother's rose bushes, always in bloom with hundreds of the scented flowers in many colours, from the palest pink to the deepest maroon; egg-yolk yellows and the purest whites.

In that primitive land, often, only mud-tracks connected one settlement to another. A trip to Tambunan, a little village in the interior, would probably have dampened the zeal of even hardened settlers. It meant a journey of several days and as Su-Moi's father's job required him to get there, the family went with him. Food, sufficient to last the whole journey, was prepared in advance. Several teams of natives and horses were organised to transport the luggage through the jungle. Su-Moi was too little to ride a horse; she was carried piggyback by a Kadazan instead. The party moved in single file. As there were no bridges spanning the rivers on the way, the men in the party would ever-so-carefully guide the horses across. Sometimes, the currents were dangerously strong, causing the men to falter in their steps, but fortunately, there were no disastrous mishaps. Each day, they would travel until they reached a resting place built by thoughtful travellers who had gone before them. At regular intervals, there would be roughly knocked-together ladders leaning against trees, at the top of which were tree-houses. Su-Moi and her family would avail themselves of these shelters as the sun began to set.

Progress in that backwater could be measured by the mode of transport: from trekking to using buffalo-carts to riding horses and bicycles. There was a limit as to how far and fast a person could go, no matter how sturdy the legs were. But there were horses aplenty in the wild, enticing the enterprising. The Yongs – Su-Moi's father and probably his brothers too – went into the jungle and rounded up five magnificent animals. Each was given an expressive and impressive Chinese name, extolling each steed's speed – names like *Fei* (fly) and *Feng* (wind).

The horses became a mode of transport at the Yongs' disposal. Horse-riding was, however, one of Su-Moi's rare failings during her life in the wild. The otherwise intrepid girl was terrified of horses, having been kicked when she once stood behind a horse to stroke it. That put her off them for life. Su-Moi's grandmother, however, worthy of her Hakka heritage and living proof of the pioneering spirit, learnt to ride a horse at the age of fifty. Seven years later, the same grandmother took to the bicycle. There she was in the clearing, trying for the umpteenth time to mount the high, unwieldy, rickety and rusty two-wheeler. Once again, she summoned her Hakka obduracy in getting the better of the machine and, after countless falls and many bruises, succeeded. Thereafter, the bicycle was her preferred mode of transport when she needed to get from plantation to plantation to visit the sick and needy.

Su-Moi's father was possibly the first person in Kudat to be the proud owner of not only horses but a carriage too. Her mother would go to church every Sunday, sitting prettily in a horse-drawn carriage. Su-Moi was enchanted by the sight, but she suspected there was many an envious eye cast in her mother's direction. Not all settlers could tame horses. It was a special gift to be able to communicate with the spirited animals, and Su-Moi's father seemed particularly talented in this. It was as if he could speak the horses' language. No wild pony was too difficult for him to tame or train. Not surprisingly, he was a first-class equestrian and polo-player. In North Borneo, he often played the game with officers of British warships which docked in the ports. Later on, he was instrumental in starting a turf club for pony racing. Later still, in 1947, when he was in Singapore, he became the first Chinese to receive a racehorse trainer's licence from the Malayan Racing Association. In 1957, he was the champion trainer.

In the vast untamed land of North Borneo, the population

was widely scattered, aggravating the lack of medical facilities and qualified medical personnel. Even practitioners of Chinese traditional medicine were not easily available; the nearest herbalist could be several kilometres away. Often, families of the sick would rely on what could euphemistically be categorised as 'alternative medicine'. Thus, when Su-Moi's aunt – then a teenager – fell ill, the only help came from some elderly women of a neighbouring plantation. They purported to be all-knowing; there was no dearth of diagnoses and prescriptions to treat the girl, delirious with typhoid fever. One treatment tried involved the slaughter of a chicken – not to make a nutritious tonic – it had to do with the feathers. These were boiled; then the boiled feathers were wrapped in a piece of black calico. (Why black? No one explained.) An egg was boiled separately. Then the patient's chest was rubbed with the poultice of feathers. After that, it was rubbed again vigorously with the boiled egg. Now the revelation: when that egg was broken, there should be hair on its yolk – presumably testimony to the success of the treatment.

Su-Moi did not get to see for herself if there was hair on the yolk used to treat her aunt. She was sent to collect the necessary ingredients for another treatment, in case the patient did not respond to the first method. The second one would have put the poor patient through far worse than mere rubbing; it involved imbibing. Manure from the buffaloes in the fields would be needed. Su-Moi, then about ten years old, was told to go with an aunt of about her age to look for a buffalo. They must make it move its bowels and when it was all done, collect the last bits of the droppings. These were for making a potion for the patient. But Su-Moi did not get to find out the potency of this cure since she and her aunt failed to persuade a single buffalo to cooperate.

But more often, for children down with fever, only spiders would be needed. The huge variety with big bodies would be right. Practitioners of folk medicine – mostly elderly women – would expertly squeeze each spider's swollen body, forcing out a liquid which, when a sufficient quantity had been obtained, was fed to the ailing child. Other insects came in handy too. Like cockroaches – perhaps for asthma. There was no shortage of these. And then there were the wild herbs. Most settlers planted some of the commonly used herbs for home cures and as seasoning in the cooking pot. For toothaches, the cure came from the kitchen. Just boil some porridge, let it cool, then put it on the affected side of the face. Su-Moi's brother, Kon Vui, had first-hand experience of this treatment. Perhaps that inspired him to dedicate his adult life to helping others with such pains in a more scientific way. He became a dentist who was especially good with children.

Su-Moi reckons that most of the cures must surely have worked well, considering her paternal grandparents' record. Of the eleven children they brought into the world, they lost just one. And it was not because of illness that this child failed to see adulthood either. He fell off a tree and died. It was her grandparents who saw her through malaria. (In that wild country, mosquitoes would emerge in vengeful swarms. One could actually hear them coming as day gave way to night.) Quinine was mixed with egg white, then rolled into little pellets, to be taken thrice a day. Su-Moi must have taken hundreds of these home-made pills. The disease would linger for a long time, tormenting the victim with severe recurring headaches. For Su-Moi, it took all of four years to be finally rid of those crippling pains.

There were, of course, severe limitations to what folk medicine could do and everyone knew what the lack of proper medical facilities could result in. Even midwives were a rarity in that land. When SuMoi's mother had her children, the only assistance she had came from an elderly woman whose only credential was that she had had children herself.

By the age of about ten, Su-Moi had outgrown her grandfather's little schoolhouse in the settlement. It was time for her to leave the familiarity of her grandparents' home for the new, to seek knowledge, to broaden her mind and to study in the English language. The elder Yongs were aware that literacy in English would make all the difference in the world; everyone noticed that the

English-literate were the ones who got good jobs. Su-Moi was very fortunate to have such enlightened parents and grandparents who believed unwaveringly in educating both the girls and the boys. Most of the Yongs' friends and neighbours shook their heads. Their usual refrain was: "Why bother to have girls educated? Sooner or later, they would belong to other families. It's downright wasteful and foolish to spend money educating girls." But the Yongs were firm in their conviction that girls too should be educated.

To give Su-Moi an English education, she was enrolled in St Monica's, a mission school in Sandakan, as a boarder. The long trip there took a day and a night by boat. The sea was quite rough at times but Su-Moi took the journey in her stride. She was to spend practically the whole decade of the 1920s at St Monica's, returning home for school vacation twice a year. School records show that Su-Moi's status as a pupil of St Monica's commenced in 1921; from 1927 to 1929, she continued to study, but at the same time taught the lower standards of the school.

At St Monica's, the missionaries had problems with Asian names finding them all tongue-twisters. To make it easier for themselves, they drew up a list of appropriate Christian names and every girl was asked to choose one for herself. Su-Moi chose Elizabeth and outside of the family, that was to be her name from henceforth. When she arrived, there was already a familiar face there – her aunt Hok-Chin, or Jessie as she chose to be known – one of her father's six younger sisters and just a few months older than she.

Elizabeth was gregarious and made new friends easily. Thus, she got on fabulously with the other boarders, some fifty in all. Much harder was learning to speak English. The boarders would inevitably prattle away in Hakka, which certainly did not help them in acquiring the English language. The teachers devised means to punish those caught speaking in other tongues than English, but it was not much of a success. By and large, the girls were obedient and stayed out of trouble, though once in a while, one of them would get into a spot. There was, for instance, the girl who was thrashed for using vulgar words. A common punishment was to limit the naughty girl to a plate of plain rice with just salt for dinner. It was hardly painful.

Reminiscing on her years at St Monica's, Elizabeth had very fond memories of the school, especially of the missionaries. The school itself, in comparison to what she later found in Singapore, was rather primitive. All the classes were under one roof, in a single-storey building. The principal would do her share of the teaching alongside the handful of teachers. Supervision of teaching was yet unknown.

In that simple setting, the missionaries influenced Elizabeth greatly. She saw in them selflessness, dedication and compassion. Elizabeth felt inspired by them. She had no difficulty adapting to the ways of this Anglican Mission[1], going to church thrice every Sunday: morning, mid-day and in the evening.

It wasn't all studies and sermons for the girls. They were given chores to do, both indoors and outdoors, much like in the settlements. The girls trimmed the lawns; chopped wood and carried water; they were also expected to do their share of housekeeping, sweeping and scrubbing the schoolhouse and the dormitories. Many of them resented these chores, but no one dared to rebel. There was one 'chore' that Elizabeth enjoyed doing: gardening. She was obviously rather good at it as, before long, she became the unofficial gardener at St Monica's. Later, as a teacher at St Andrew's in Singapore, she would be the one to go to school on weekends and during school vacation to tend the school garden.

In retrospect, Elizabeth is grateful for the spartan way of life at St Monica's. If she first arrived a sturdy girl, by the time she left, she was even more hardy and rugged. And athletic: "Whenever I took part in sports, I always took the first prize." Perhaps life in the jungle had something to do with developing the latent athletic prowess of the Yongs. Her brother, Kon Vui, was the athletics champion for each of his five years as a dental student at Singapore's King Edward VII College of Medicine. Even her youngest sister, Marie, who had only spent her first year of life in Borneo, turned out to be quite an athlete, proving her mettle during her days at the Teachers' Training

College in Singapore.

The missionary teachers concentrated on moulding their young charges into good Christian girls. Much of the goings-on in the world were sieved out as irrelevant. Loyalty to the English Crown was limited to singing 'God Save the King' – to the school children it was just an anthem, nothing more; it certainly did not fire patriotism for the English monarch. A little geography was taught but no history. (The missionaries were not biased: no history of the Middle Kingdom and no enlightenment on the British Empire either.) And definitely no politics of any kind. But the missionaries did teach the girls not to get mixed up with boys – not even by correspondence; not even when one was related to the other. A girl who was caught writing to a boy-cousin in a boys' school was punished. Every girl was warned that she should keep away from boys in public, which included church. During services, boys would be seated on one side of the hall and girls on the other. To Elizabeth, it was very much like the parish church in Kudat where the menfolk were segregated from the womenfolk across the aisle. In the streets, if the girls spotted boys passing by, they would swiftly turn their faces the other way. It was the proper thing to do.

The missionaries were surrogate parents to the girls. They were always available to listen to any troubled child and never failed to give advice and reassurance in moments of difficulty or doubt. A favourite practice was quoting appropriate verses from the Bible to uplift the girls' spirits. Elizabeth's retentive mind kept those quotes in store and, for years after, found strength in the words first uttered by these missionaries. The girls were also encouraged to go for confession. There was no coercion but should any of them need a listening ear, the priest would be there. It would be a face-to-face exchange.

Elizabeth found that each time she went to confession, she would come away feeling much lighter in heart. Once, she had gone in search of solace and advice when Archdeacon Bernard Mercer said to her: "God has given you special graces and you must make use of those graces." In the years ahead, as an adult, whenever she faced tribulations, what the Archdeacon had said to her would come to mind.

St Monica's principal, Miss Anne Rigby, was another source of inspiration. She worked exceedingly hard in running the school and watched over her girls very carefully, noting the strengths and weaknesses of each. In Elizabeth's school-leaving testimonial of November 1929, Miss Rigby took note of her "intelligence and initiative" and went on to state that Elizabeth "is in every way reliable and a good influence wherever she goes." To this, Archdeacon Mercer added a note on Elizabeth's "sterling character." The words in the two testimonials were a source of great encouragement to the teenager and fortified her as she embarked on the next phase of her life – in Singapore.

However, it was in Singapore that she was to face her first blow. When Elizabeth was there, her mother had her sixth child. In her debilitated state after childbirth, she fell victim to cerebral malaria and died when the baby was just three days old. Elizabeth was stunned when she learnt of her mother's death as she had not been aware of her poor health and illness. As the eldest child, she understood instinctively that she should look after her younger brothers and sisters. She made a silent promise to her departed mother that she would be her siblings' protector, especially the newborn sister she had yet to meet; she would be there for them, to see them through thick and thin, to help them realise their full potential.

In the years ahead, Elizabeth's memories of her mother remained vividly fresh; it was as if she had never left. In times of distress, she would talk to her and feel comforted and reassured. As for the promise she made to care for her siblings, she would keep it faithfully, despite the sacrifices she would have to make.

---

1   Su-Moi's family was initiated into the rituals of the Basel Mission which was closely allied with the Lutheran Church.

III

AN ANGLO CATHOLIC

SINGAPORE: The place for people of North Borneo in search of higher education and better career prospects. It was relatively easy getting there. No passports were needed. No formalities. Just get on a boat headed that way. Seven days on the high seas at the cost of a few dollars. That was all it took.

It was December 1929 when the steamer S. S. *Darvel* brought Elizabeth, chaperoned by her grandmother, to Singapore. Other members of the Yong family had gone before her. Her fifth aunt, Jessie, was already studying in Singapore when Elizabeth arrived. A Chee Swee Cheng scholarship holder, Aunt Jessie was the first pupil groomed by St Monica's for the Cambridge School Certificate examination. The Convent of the Holy Infant Jesus in Singapore was pleased to have Jessie as a pupil.

Elizabeth's academic results had been excellent throughout her years at St Monica's. She often competed with Aunt Jessie in scholastic performance and at times, Elizabeth had the better of her aunt. They both sat for the test to qualify for the Chee Swee Cheng scholarship offered by a community leader of that name in Malaya. But the test covered many subjects, including mathematics, Elizabeth's Achilles' heel. Her mark for that subject pulled down her average score and she failed to obtain the scholarship. But her thirst for greater knowledge was obvious to her parents and they wanted her to realise her full potential. Thus, the year after the departure of her aunt, Elizabeth too left for Singapore.

The Borneons visualised Singapore as a place of sophistication. Elizabeth's parents did not want their daughter to look or feel out of place when she arrived in Singapore. All the female Yongs had kept their hair long, neatly braided into plaits. (When they were very young, all of them had the front portion of their heads shaven, but the back long and plaited, much like the hairstyle of men of the Qing Dynasty.) Her parents assumed plaits were too old fashioned for a big town, but where they were, there were no beauty parlour to take care of women's coiffure. They made do with what was available: a barber. He cropped Elizabeth's hair right up her nape – and more, several centimetres more.

By then, Elizabeth had grown into a broad-shouldered lanky lass of 1.68 metres. Tall indeed for a Chinese woman but her parents hailed from large-framed stock. (Elizabeth recalled her mother was about the same height as she.) When Aunt Jessie set eyes on her in Singapore, the sight of the statuesque Elizabeth with her cropped hair was a bit too much. It was clear that she did not want to be associated with this manly country bumpkin of a niece. She told Elizabeth loud and clear that she should keep at least five metres behind her.

Singapore was a whole new world to Elizabeth. For the girl from the jungles of North Borneo, her reaction to Singapore was "Wow!" However, there was little time to be captivated by her new environment. There were pressing matters of settling down to attend to. By the time Elizabeth left St Monica's, she had long overcome her earlier difficulty and hesitation in speaking English. But a simple question asked of her left her dumbfounded: her birth date. Elizabeth had never been asked that before. And she didn't know! She had to write home for that vital bit of personal information. It took some time for the reply to arrive: 1912, the first of May. And this was duly entered into the school's records. Later, she learnt that she was in fact older than that; she had been given her younger sister's birth date by mistake! She was actually born in 1910, on the 29th of November.

There was a similar mistake with a brother; like Elizabeth, he was given a sibling's birth date. In the years ahead, it took some time and effort to unravel all those mixed-up dates. They were of course born in the days when it was not mandatory to report births and deaths to the authorities. Thus, much depended on the memories of older members of the family. For Elizabeth, officially, she remains one year five months and two days younger than she actually is.[1]

Elizabeth had already been told before leaving for Singapore that the convent which had welcomed Aunt Jessie had no vacancy for her. However, there was a place for her in another mission school. But a strange twist of events – triggered by her aunt's cowardice – led to the convent offering Elizabeth a place after all.

Despite Aunt Jessie's unfailingly brilliant academic results year after year, she could not bring herself to go to school for her Senior Cambridge examination results. She turned to her niece Elizabeth for help, asking her to go to the convent and get her results from the principal.

In those days, the examination papers were marked and graded in Penang. The results would be posted on the school's notice-board on Christmas Day. To go to the convent and ask for her aunt's results – whatever the day – was not a task Elizabeth would have volunteered for. (Elizabeth was awed by the convent in Victoria Street, so vastly unlike St Monica's, so large, so many students – more than a thousand – and so many teachers, mostly nuns from France and Ireland.) But she could not refuse her nerve-stricken aunt.

So, off she went and found the principal, Madam St Columban. The nun took her down a long corridor and asked many questions of Elizabeth. She answered each question politely and told the principal that, yes, she too had come to Singapore to study but there was no place for her in the convent. The principal told her that the convent set "very high standards". Elizabeth accepted that. But on her way out after having obtained her aunt's results – she had passed with flying colours; in fact, she was the convent's dux for that year – the principal asked Elizabeth: "Would you like to come to this school?" There could only be one answer from the astonished and delighted girl: "Yes!" And she was in.

And so Elizabeth, brought up as a Lutheran, schooled as an Anglican at St Monica's, now found herself in a Roman Catholic convent. But it posed no problem to her. On her own volition, she would attend mass. This was noticed by some of the nuns. One of them who knew she had come from St Monica's and therefore assumed her to be non-Catholic, asked: "Why don't you become a Catholic?" Elizabeth's disarming reply was: "I am a Catholic. Only I am an Anglo Catholic, not a Roman Catholic."

While her piety withstood the test of time and was unwavering, Elizabeth was one of the most liberated and tolerant persons in matters of religion. Even as a youngster, she instinctively believed that it really did not matter whether the person was an Anglican, a Lutheran, a Baptist, a Presbyterian, a Catholic or what have you. As an adult, she was convinced that it truly does not matter whether the person is a Christian, a Buddhist, a Hindu or a Muslim or a follower of any other religion. To her, all religions lead to God, although her only religion is Christianity. Her lodestar: "Do good and abhor evil."

Like her aunt, Elizabeth shone for her family and her country of origin. The principal was so pleased with the performance of the Yongs of North Borneo that she asked whether there were more girls in Borneo wanting to study in Singapore![2] Elizabeth was an exemplary student but there were nevertheless obstacles to the perfect score. She felt particularly inadequate during her first year. There were tears of frustration aplenty each night.

Mathematics, in particular, tortured her. She noticed that others did not seem at all confounded by all those perplexing mathematical problems which she found bewildering. She could not accept that perhaps she was not born for figures and was determined to overcome her difficulty with this subject. Thus, she bought a copy of the *Workman's Arithmetic* which provided answers at the back. When she was through with her homework for the day, she would work at the problems in this book, trying again and again until she not only got the answers right but understood the logical steps involved in solving each problem. It took three months of stubborn pursuit, each night working till midnight by a small light. That probably was when she spoilt her eyesight but, to her, no price was too great to prove she could do it. The final triumph was to sail through mathematics in the Senior Cambridge examination. It was such sweet reward.

In Singapore, Elizabeth and Aunt Jessie stayed upstairs in a double-storey shophouse along Selegie Road which belonged to her father's brother, her fourth uncle.[3] Instead of being cloistered in the flat, Elizabeth and her aunt would seek the outdoors by going up Mount Emily each evening with their books to study. The lush greenery, the flora, the majestic trees and not least of all, the serenity and quietness of the place, were probably very much like home in North Borneo.

Elizabeth recalls the traffic – or the lack of it – in those days. There were just a few motorised vehicles seen on the narrow roads of the town, outnumbered by buffalo-carts and horse-carriages, providing transport along with rickshaws and bicycles. And yes, buses had arrived in Singapore. These were trolley-buses powered by overhead cables. Elizabeth would stand on the road-side and watch the bus driver negotiate tricky junctions. The conductor would hop off the bus, pull the pulleys off the wires overhead, then reconnect them again after the bus had made the necessary turn. A laborious process. There were also the mosquito-buses, each able to ferry seven passengers. Later came the yellow-top taxis. Traffic jams belonged to the future. People used their legs a great deal. To Elizabeth, having walked practically daily over long distances through jungle treks, walking in Singapore was a breeze. When there was time, she would even walk, or cycle, all the way to Johor Baru on the peninsula to the north of Singapore.

Elizabeth looked forward to the school holidays, when she

would have more time for the orphans at the convent whom pupils were encouraged to help look after and befriend. Many of these children were not strictly orphans but were abandoned at the convent doorstep, probably by destitute and desperate parents who could not afford to feed another mouth. Most of the abandoned children were girls; some were disabled. There were no social services to help families which could not make ends meet in those days, nor were there family planners to advise the adults how not to bring unwanted babies to this world. The parents who left their infants outside the convent's door knew that the nuns would look after them much better than they themselves could. Elizabeth adored the children and enjoyed playing with them. She would save her pocket-money to buy them little gifts and, when she had time, to sew clothes for them. Seeing their smiling faces gave Elizabeth a sense of usefulness and purpose.

Her own first year at the convent passed quickly. Elizabeth must have been the happiest person the day in December 1930 when she received the convent's Prize of Honour, the very first girl from North Borneo to win the special award. The prize was for the most outstanding student, in studies and in character. The medal bore the school's motto in French, meaning: "Simple in virtue; strong in duty." A mark of Elizabeth's character had become discernible by then: not only did she display an almost childlike delight in mottos and compliments, she also felt a strong compulsion to live up to them. So too, an almost obsessive urge to do things the "missionary way" – as she put it – and to seek altruism in her actions. These traits remained long after she had left her school days behind.

One can imagine her father's pleasure and pride on learning of his eldest child's success when he went to Singapore to visit her at the end of that first year. But he had gone alone. So, Elizabeth asked her father to take the medal she had won and the prize, a large King's dictionary, back to Kudat to show her mother. The vision of her mother waving goodbye to her as she left for Singapore a year earlier remained fresh in Elizabeth's memory; so too the tug at her heartstrings which she had felt. She was not to know then that that would be the last time she would ever see her mother, who died not long after her father's visit. She was just forty-one years old. Elizabeth was all the more glad that she had given her prize and medal to her father to take to her, so that she could share her daughter's achievement and be reassured that her firstborn was doing well and that she could be proud of her.

Elizabeth ably sustained her sparkling performance at the convent for the next two years. At the end of her third year, she sat for the Senior Cambridge examination. Her result: the dux of the convent. She would have dearly loved to further her studies at Raffles College[4] – her laudable performance should have ensured her not only a place but, very possibly, a scholarship as well. But alas, her academic ambitions were dashed by the onslaught of the Great Depression.

Of the countries in the world, those dependent on commodities and trade were among the worst hit. Indeed, their vulnerability was severely exposed during the catastrophic years of the worst slump in the world's history. The depression had in fact had a stranglehold on the economies of the West the year Elizabeth left North Borneo for Singapore, in 1929. It took time for the impact to be felt by countries away from the epicentre of the economic disaster. While Elizabeth was single-mindedly in pursuit of academic excellence, the economies of Singapore and the Malayan Peninsula were among those crumbling from the epochal depression. The twin principles of free trade and free immigration which had sustained the economies of British colonies and protectorates fell casualty to the slump. Singapore's prosperity was trade-based, especially of commodities. It was a fact that Singapore rode on the back of Malaya's rubber and tin: the famed twin pillars of the Malayan economy.

With the depression in the West came a devastating shrinkage in demand for commodities; as demand shrank, prices dived. The price of natural rubber: from an average of 34 cents (Straits Settlement currency) in 1929 to 4.95 cents in mid-1932. Tin went through the same plunge, with demand dropping by over 40 per cent during the slump.[5]

In the streets of Singapore, an island of shopkeepers and traders, there were visible signs that all was far from well. Instead of the normal hive of activity, there was eerie inactivity. Rows of shops – such as those of the previously bustling High Street, South Bridge Road and North Bridge Road – were shuttered. On many a tightly-shut shopfront was the tell-tale sign: 'to Let'. In both the public and private sectors, those who were lucky enough not to be retrenched had to accept pay cuts. Civil service pay shrank by one-fifth. The government, unable to balance its budget, found it prudent to slash its expenditure, to the extent of temporarily suspending scholarships to Raffles College.

The Yongs in North Borneo could not possibly escape the all-engulfing repercussions of the depression. Like other settlers who had put their faith in the land, the fruit of their labour was now practically worthless. As far as Elizabeth was concerned, she did not forget that she was the eldest of her parents' six children. There were the younger ones to educate. And there was her promise to her mother. She could not go to college. And so it was to work.

---

1   Schools then were not strict about age limits of students. In Elizabeth's class in Singapore, some of her classmates were five years younger than she.

2   This soon led to the arrival of Elizabeth's youngest aunt, her father's youngest sister. Unfortunately, the latest Yong girl's academic performance was not on par with the earlier arrivals. But she got through and went on to pursue a nursing career.

3   This uncle too had gone to China for further studies. But unlike Elizabeth's father and his second brother who went there to acquire Chinese literacy, he went to Shanghai to study English. Upon completion of his education in Shanghai, he went to work in Singapore.

4   This evolved into the Singapore-based University of Malaya in 1949.

5   Overall the volume of international trade in 1933 – considered the end of the depression – was barely a third of what it had been in 1929. What the British administration did to counter the slump was unprecedented: not only did they implement immigration curbs on the Chinese, there was also repatriation of Chinese and Indians. In 1931, a historic and dismal year, for the first time, emigrants outnumbered immigrants. This trend would prevail in the next two years. With the introduction of imperial preferential tariffs and quotas in 1932, the British had turned its back on the principle of free trade.

IV

A NOBLE CALLING

WHEN ELIZABETH reconciled herself to the reality before her, – that college would be out of the question – teaching became the obvious career choice. She wanted to be properly trained to teach and guide young minds, but the normal classes for the training of teachers had ceased at that time. So her change in status, from student to teacher, was without the transitory training phase.

The first school she taught at was St Margaret's – then known by the initialism CEZMS (Church of England Zenana Mission School) – Singapore's first girls' school, founded in 1842. Her Aunt Jessie was also a teacher at this school. Aunt and niece were delighted that a Girl Guides company was being set up at the school when they became members of the teaching staff. They eagerly signed up. Back at St Monica's in North Borneo, the twosome had been the first girls to join the movement there. (Elizabeth joined the First North Borneo Guide Company at its inauguration in 1925. She had served as second class guide, patrol leader and then as company leader.) Throughout her life, Elizabeth would highly recommend movements like the Girl Guides, Boy Scouts and Boys' Brigade. Such activities, she pointed out, would help train and mould the young in their formative and impressionable years, to grow up right.

Elizabeth remained at St Margaret's for two years. Then came an offer to teach at St Andrew's School which she accepted. She was aware that she was the only teacher in the school without formal teacher training. (She was to receive normal training later while holding her teaching post.) But the principal of St Andrew's, Canon Reginald Keith Sorby Adams, and her colleagues soon put her at ease. Canon Adams made light of her diffidence and instilled confidence in her; at the same time, he inspired her with his own dedication. He, more than anyone else, reassured Elizabeth that she had made a perfect career choice; he, more than anyone else, made St Andrew's a joyful place of work for Elizabeth. Elizabeth was captivated by him and retained fond memories of the former principal.[1] The environment at St Andrew's was so congenial, her love of teaching so great, that no other job offer could tempt her to leave.

Elizabeth was a natural with children; she was an exceptionally gifted teacher. Without any formal training, she demonstrated her instinctive understanding of children. To her, it all seemed like so much common sense. She believed unwaveringly that all children, even the naughty ones, really want to be good, that it is very important that teachers do not hold back words of praise, to encourage the children who are trying to do even better. She frowned upon punishing children, even if just verbal reprimand. Or worse, to frighten a child in any way. Her way was to look for the good in the child and to build on it. To her, there should be no bias in the treatment of children, whatever the race or religion, whatever the economic standing of the individual child's family. Throughout her teaching years, she adhered to this. Schools, she noted, are the perfect place where multi-racialism can be effectively practised and mutual acceptance and tolerance inculcated in the children from young. And teachers are vitally important in setting the right examples before their pupils.

At St Andrew's, Elizabeth became so well-known for her ability in getting naughty schoolboys to behave and co-operate that she would be the depository of pupils other teachers found too much of a handful. Elizabeth attributed her understanding of children, her patience in dealing with them, to the kindness she received from the adults around her during her own childhood. If she deemed appropriate, Elizabeth would visit the families of boys who had problems – the difficult ones as well as the slow learners. She found it important to understand the family background of the boys under her charge. Almost without fail, her own theory and suspicion would be confirmed when she noticed the difficult ones, the emotionally disturbed, would inevitably be those from broken homes. By and large, she found the parents co-operative and appreciative of her efforts.

Elizabeth the teacher would have cut quite a formidable figure to the little primary schoolboys. She had the carriage of a professional soldier. She could be stern when the occasion called for it, but her kindness would always show through. Teaching, to her, is a calling – a very noble calling. A teacher, she said, is a very privileged person. "When the best is given, the children know it and they and their parents will always be grateful to you; a teacher's caring and unselfish attitude endears her or him to the children. It's a very satisfying feeling." She went beyond her duties as a teacher in doing her best to nurture the young. Not only in terms of extra time spent with those having difficulties in keeping up with the rest of the class in lessons, but in material help too – if she thought it necessary.

The carefully hand-written thank you notes in block lettering from the little boys she taught meant as much to her as the formally typed and signed missives from grateful parents. In her retirement, ever so often, some well-dressed professional young or not-so-young man would come up to greet her. She, of course, would not be able to put names to faces. But no matter. The men would always introduce themselves and inform her that they had been in her class in such-and-such a year. Such encounters never failed to give Elizabeth a special glow of satisfaction. It was, she asserted, much better than additional zeros to the pay cheque.

Measured in terms of monetary returns, the teaching profession was hardly the most rewarding choice. During her many years as a teacher, she had seen all too many colleagues leave for greener pastures and had indeed prospered by the change of career. But to her, the intangible rewards – the satisfaction, esteem and affection – these far outweighed monetary rewards. Even within the teaching profession, there were opportunities beckoning. In the post-war years, there were offers aplenty, to entice her to other schools, offering her more money and higher status in the school hierarchy. (There was a dire shortage of English-educated teachers during that time as the government had changed its pre-war hands-off education policy to one which offered each child a place in school.) But no, not only did Elizabeth love teaching, she was devoted to St Andrew's.

In 1956, Canon Adams, by then based in Kucing, Sarawak, wrote a testimonial on Elizabeth (by then Mrs Choy) whom he remembered well, as she sought leave from St Andrew's to take up the post of principal of the School for the Blind:

> *Not only has her teaching been skilled, but from the first, even before she received her training in teaching, she showed a love and leadership among small children that gave them so much more than material knowledge. Her warm sympathy with them enabled her from the outset to build up in them values that I have seen come to fruition in her pupils as they grew up. It was always a joy to watch Mrs Choy at work with her 'family', which her class inevitably became.*

Mrs Choy's appointment as the first principal of the School for the Blind had much to do with her dedication to social work. As the pioneer principal of the school, it meant starting very much from scratch, right down to finding the disabled – to enrol them as students – and to having teachers trained to teach the blind. She relished the challenge offered her. Here she stayed till 1960. By then, the school had taken proper shape and had become accepted as the place where visually-impaired children could receive proper training to enable them to lead independent lives in their adulthood.

Then it was back again to the children at St Andrew's.

There she remained till the end of the 1974 school year. On 25 February 1975, some 1,500 teachers, pupils and friends gathered to attend a farewell party for Mrs Choy. It was goodbye to St Andrew's Junior School and the career of her choice, teaching: "The noblest, most difficult but most satisfying profession." In 1979, she was invited as the guest-of-honour at the school's 117th Founder's Day. It was a break from tradition; a bold move by the principal, Mr Harry Tan, to choose a woman for the event. Mrs Choy was deeply touched by the gesture and was very moved by the occasion. She was perhaps the first guest-of-honour who had tears streaming down her cheeks while taking the salute from the uniformed units. She recognised some members of the guard-of-honour. The chubby-cheeked little boys of primary three or four whom she had taught now stood taller, resplendent in their starched uniforms. She was so proud of each and everyone of them. When she addressed the gathering, she had no script; she spoke from her heart, of the splendid fulfilment she had as a teacher.

Along with the joy of teaching was the joy of learning. Elizabeth's thirst for knowledge was insatiable. After the war, she would grasp every opportunity to learn more, and yet more. Her four years in Britain in the immediate post-war years were not just for recuperation and relaxation. During that time, she made the best use possible of the available facilities to learn. Returning to her teaching job in Singapore, she would find yet more courses to attend. And she proudly kept the stack of certificates of attendance issued by the then University of Singapore under its extension course programme for adults: in world politics, educational sociology, vocational guidance; on Singapore, South-east Asia, Malaysia, Japan and more.

There were loud moans among many civil servants, including teachers, when Malay became Singapore's national language. For most of them, it meant learning a new language; they resented having to do so. But not so Mrs Choy. She was enthusiastic and devoted many hours mastering it, reading *Berita Harian*, the news daily in Malay, to expand her vocabulary and improve her usage of the language. She passed all the examinations, right up to Standard III level. In the process, she was rewarded, earning a total of $700: $200 for passing Standard II, another $500 for the next level. She went on to win prizes in the language. In 1964, by then a deputy principal of St Andrew's Junior School, she won first prize in one contest and took the second prize in another. She progressed to the Higher School Certificate level and passed the oral test but did not sit for the written paper. Her ambition to be literate in the Jawi script was dampened when she failed the Standard III examination in Jawi. She was then about sixty years old: "I felt very bad because it was the first examination I ever failed."

The next decade, the 1970s, Mrs Choy tackled the Chinese language. By then, what she had learnt as a child was largely lost. She attended classes run by a commercial school in Prinsep Street; when government-run courses were available, she switched to those. In 1971, she passed the Adult Education Board's elementary Chinese. In the following year, it was the Ministry of Education's Standard I special examination in the Chinese language. Despite these encouraging successes, her lack of confidence in speaking Mandarin proficiently deterred her from further pursuit.

Elizabeth, as the oldest child, was a filial daughter to her father and a devoted surrogate mother to her siblings. She felt a special commitment to her youngest sister, Marie Su-Tshin, who was just three days old when their mother died. Their paternal grandmother took care of the baby in Borneo. When Marie was a year old, she was sent to Singapore where Elizabeth took over the responsibility of bringing her up. There were also four other younger siblings. Elizabeth was determined to help her father put them all through school. Thus, she refused to consider marriage although she had a suitor by the time she left the convent.

When Elizabeth was in the convent, she had a classmate named Florence. Elizabeth would often walk her home for lunch. (In those days, lessons were spread over the whole day with a lunch break.) 'Home' for Florence was that of her guardians, a Choy family from Hongkong. She was, in fact, betrothed to the Choys' eldest son.

Florence's future mother-in-law took a liking to the well-mannered and courteous Elizabeth, making her feel very welcome. Knowing that Elizabeth's parents were not in Singapore, she insisted on Elizabeth having lunch with her before returning to school. The appreciative Elizabeth did not realise then that the elderly woman – a mother of four sons and four daughters – had designs on her: as a daughter-in-law, the wife for her second son! Florence did her best to get Elizabeth interested. But Elizabeth's mind was not on romance or on the building of a nest of her own. Her priorities remained unchanged: to do her part in seeing her siblings through their education.

However, as she recounted years later, she relented because she could not bear to see the elderly woman's disappointment. She convinced herself that it would be the right thing to do – "typical of my missionary upbringing" – to make the mother happy by agreeing to the marriage. But her future husband would have to wait, until such time as Elizabeth felt was right for her to get married. And wait he did – for almost ten years.

It was on 16 August 1941 when Elizabeth Yong Su-Moi, aged thirty-one, took the name Choy. It was a double wedding. Her brother Kon Vui, who had by then qualified as a dental surgeon, tied the knot that very day too. The two brides, Elizabeth and Maureen, were dressed in identical gowns, intriguingly described by a news reporter as: "Plastic white angel skin lace, styled with heart-shaped necklines, wrist-length sleeves and trains cut in one with the skirt." However, while Elizabeth wore a headdress of gardenias, Maureen's was of orange blossoms. The ceremony was held at St Andrew's Cathedral, officiated by Archdeacon Graham White and assisted by Canon Adams.

The Yongs of North Borneo sailed in in full force to witness Elizabeth's long-awaited marriage, rendered doubly memorable by the double wedding. Four hundred guests were invited to the reception. The Victoria Memorial Hall, just a short walk from the Cathedral, was one of the few places which could accommodate such a large gathering. And so it was at the Victoria Memorial Hall where the wedding reception took place. It was a joyous occasion. The gregarious Yongs indulged in the pleasure of each others' company right through the honeymoon. There were at least a dozen of them in the wedding party that went touring the peninsula, enjoying the seaside of Mersing, Johor, together with the newly-weds.

Who among the happy gathering of family-members and well-wishers had any premonition that the world as they knew it would soon vanish? Who among them could have foreseen the calamity ahead? Who could have known then that in just six months, the British would abandon the Empire's vaunted and prized Far East naval base – Singapore – the supposedly impregnable and invincible fortress? But it did come to pass. On 15 February 1942, at the Ford factory in Upper Bukit Timah Road, victorious Japan's Lieutenant-General Tomoyuki Yamashita would accept defeated Britain's Lieutenant-General Arthur E. Percival's unconditional surrender.

About a month before the surrender, as tension mounted by the day, as an invasion by the Japanese had become ominously imminent, all schools were closed. Some, like St Andrew's, were converted into casualty centres for victims of Japanese bombing and shelling. Business activities ground to a halt. Evacuation of civilian expatriates and others was in full swing. For the newly-wed Choys, personal tragedy befell them even before the fall of the island. Six weeks after the Japanese dropped the first bomb on Singapore, Elizabeth suffered a miscarriage. The benumbed couple faced their future together with trepidation.

---

1   "What's your race?" "Why, the human race of course." That would be a typical Canon Adams answer. An Australian by birth, Elizabeth recalled he was a true all-rounder: "A great scholar and a sportsman; he was a very liberal and yet committed missionary; a linguist as well – among the tongues he mastered was Malay. Along with his sense of humour was his humility. There was none of the uppity colonial attitude in him."

V

DOUBLE TENTH

DOUBLE TENTH. The historic day when China's victorious Kuomintang consigned the last of the Qing Dynasty to ignominy and history, leading to the official birth of the Republic of China on the first day of 1912. And to this day, this Double Tenth is celebrated with aplomb yearly, on the island of Taiwan.

Lesser known is another 'Double Tenth', that of 1943. It was the day the Japanese sought vengeance in Singapore for the daring destruction of seven ships in Singapore's Keppel Harbour on 27 September. The Japanese failed to track down the saboteurs despite their thorough search of the waters around Singapore. They desperately needed to pin the treachery on some culprits, to punish them. The heroism of the saboteurs is well documented. They were a team of just fourteen – Force Z – led by Ivan Lyon, then a captain. A member of the Gordan Highlanders, he was responsible for the evacuation of refugees fleeing Singapore. Tragically, his own wife and son failed to get away. Thus, he was seen as a person with a personal score to settle. But he was more than a driven seeker of vengeance; he inspired others with his leadership. He had meticulously planned the attack, selected and trained his men for the gruelling mission.

Dubbed Operation Jaywick – the fact that that was the name of a popular brand of caustic toilet detergent was no coincidence – the mission was under the command of the Special Operations Executive (Far East). A fishing boat renamed *Krait* – as in snake – was repaired and made ready for the operation. Among its cargo were canoes and limpet mines.

Stained brown and clad in sarongs, the fourteen saboteurs looked native enough at a safe distance. They lay in wait south of Singapore, at Indonesia's Panjang Island. When the time was judged right, the saboteurs, two per canoe, approached their heavily-guarded targets and remained undetected as they stealthily carried out their deadly task. In all, they planted limpet mines on seven ships. As quietly and swiftly as they came, they left. As they rowed with all their might towards the pre-determined rendezvous at Dongas Island, the deafening explosions they heard assured them that the raid had been successful.

By 19 October 1943, Force Z was in Australia, celebrating the saboteurs' valour – and the destruction of Japanese ships, all of 37,000 tons, in Singapore waters, right under the nose and gun-barrel of the occupation forces.[1]

In Singapore, there was hell to pay. Not only were detainees in the Changi Prison internment camp singled out for Japanese vengeance, so too some hapless members of the public. Possession of radio sets was strictly forbidden by the occupation forces. But the Japanese had for some time suspected that those incarcerated in Changi were not only receiving information over illicit wireless sets but also relaying information out of the jail to Allied forces. A plan was already afoot to raid the jail in December 1943. With the destruction of the ships in the Singapore harbour, that raid was brought forward to 10 October 1943. For most of the internees of Changi, 'Double Tenth' was their initiation to the methods of the *Kempeitai*; some would not survive the viciousness of the Japanese Military Police.

On 9 October 1943, the internees were told that there would be a roll-call the next morning. No one had any premonition of what was awaiting although, in retrospect, there were tell-tale signs. For one, there had already been a roll-call. Also, some days earlier, the jail was visited by a number of Japanese armed with building plans and measuring tapes. The Japanese professed concern for the physical well-being of the internees, taking note that the jail was overcrowded; the claim was that they wished to renovate and enlarge the quarters. No one could foresee doom. But then what could they do even if they did?

On the morning of 10 October, it became ominously clear that the last thing the Japanese had in mind was to make life more comfortable for the internees. Justice N. A. Worley, an ex-internee, wrote in 1946:

> *None of us will ever forget that parade at dawn in the main yard for roll-call, the sudden and unexpected appearance of armed sentries and of repulsive-looking men, in mufti, but armed with pistols who prowled round peering and searching everywhere. Then, as one by one, a number of leading internees were called out and segregated, and it became obvious that the visitors were "acting on information received," we realised what was afoot and the chill of fear, the premonition of danger, struck at us all.*[2]

There were indeed radio sets hidden in the prison. But these could only receive information; the internees did not have the wherewithal to transmit from Changi. On 10 October, they had not even heard of the derring-do of Force Z a fortnight earlier.

No one knew for certain how many radio sets there were in the jail. No amount of threats, torture and abuse could get the *Kempeitai* all the answers they thirsted for: on the number of pieces in operation and the people involved. What could be determined was that each set had been assembled with parts smuggled into the prison. Before Operation Jaywick, some internees had regular opportunities to drive into town as members of work parties or ambulance drivers. The Japanese sentries were not always vigilant. The internees were able to contact non-internees, to obtain the necessary parts to build radio sets.

Sometimes, go-betweens were used. Such was the case when the ethnic Indian driver of the Japanese commandant relayed a message to one S. Cornelius that the latter's former boss, by then an inmate of Changi, would like to have the components to build a radio set. It could be quite simply accomplished. Cornelius would pass the pieces to the driver, since the car was used by the commandant, it was never searched. Upon reaching the jail, the car would develop some mechanical hiccup. Then, right there in the prison camp workshop, internees who serviced military motor vehicles would take delivery of the parts and spirit them away. In the aftermath of the success of Operation Jaywick, the commandant's driver was among those who had aroused the *Kempeitai's* suspicion. He was executed; most likely after interrogation, torture and confession. Cornelius too was arrested, tortured and died at the hands of the *Kempeitai*. The recipient of the radio parts shared his fate.

Another recipient of radio parts, W. L. Stevenson was mightily attached to his stool; he carried it everywhere with him. His fellow inmates just assumed he was more than a little eccentric and, under the circumstances, who could blame him? However, it turned out that he had successfully assembled a radio set and had quite cleverly concealed it under the seat of the stool. No one realised that until the *Kempeitai* discovered it. Stevenson too died at the hands of his torturers.

Then there was John Long's set. He had occasion to drive an ambulance ferrying sick internees to the Miyako Hospital, formerly a mental institution. Not one to let such golden opportunities slip by, Long started to smuggle bits and pieces of a radio set back to the prison. He assembled his set under the medical officer's desk in the camp hospital. He too was to die at the hands of the *Kempeitai*, but not before the *Kempeitai* had learnt that his parts came from the hospital canteen operator, Choy Khun Heng, Elizabeth's husband.

1 The success of this mission doubtless encouraged the Allies to plan yet
   another attack, a far more ambitious and audacious one. Operation Rimau
   was scheduled for 10 October 1944. It was a disaster. Twenty-three Allied
   commandos were on this mission. None lived to tell.

2 *The Double Tenth Trial: War Crimes Court* edited by Bashir A. Mallal;
   foreword by Justice N.A. Worley (Malayan Law Journal, Singapore 1947)

VI

HELL AROUND THE CORNER

THE THREAT posed by the militant Japanese had seemed so remote, so unreal to Elizabeth Yong Su-Moi. The looming war in distant Europe that she read about was irrelevant to her daily life in Singapore. Although happenings in countries closer to home – like the seemingly incessant shelling of Vietnam – were reported in the newspapers, they did not trigger any political awakening in her, nor did they cause her alarm over the security of Singapore. She was just happy to be a useful person, teaching the young while helping her siblings to get educated. She had heard of the League of Nations and reckoned it was a good thing. She had taken note of the surge in Chinese nationalism in Singapore in the 1930s. Members of the ethnic Chinese community were outraged by Japanese atrocities on the mainland, in China. Japanese aggression had been emboldened by the ineptitude of the Nationalist Government, the Kuomintang, that had transformed the Kingdom of China into the Republic of China in 1912.

For China, the war with Japan officially started in 1937. It was to be one humiliating defeat after another for the Chinese armies and untold suffering for the masses. The Japanese appetite for territory was insatiable; not content with effectively nibbling away at

Manchuria, the resource-rich north-east corner of China, it wanted nothing less than the whole of China. To the Chinese of Singapore, China was still 'home'. Even the English-educated Chinese tended to look upon China as such; some more whole-heartedly than others. There were many, mostly those who spoke and were literate in the Chinese language, who desperately wanted to help protect their motherland. If they were unable to march alongside the defenders of China, they could at least marshal financial and moral support. The United China Relief Fund collected money for the cause. Black armbands were sold and worn with nationalist pride – and sorrow – displaying for all to see their patriotism and loyalty to China.

Elizabeth never doubted her own ethnicity, but the contagious anger, anguish and angst of many Chinese in Singapore seemed to leave her quite untouched. In later years, she rationalised that her detachment from the Chinese cause had much to do with the influence of missionaries in her life. Missionaries were not interested in politics.

It was not among the subjects taught or even discussed in mission schools. But in the privately-run Chinese-medium schools, the students were very much aware of world events and had access to publications which reported and discussed the political developments in China in Chinese, a language which had become quite foreign to Elizabeth by then. Nor were Elizabeth and her family in touch with relatives living in the land of their forebears. Thus, they were not directly exposed to the despair spilled through letters from China.

Be that as it may, Elizabeth and her family were not exceptional in their faith in the British. They – and there were many others who believed likewise – never doubted for a moment that the British would valiantly defend Singapore and be victorious. But alas, it had been a fools' paradise. The Japanese seemed unstoppable at that stage of military aggression as their armies advanced into Indochina and South-east Asia.

To those who hung on to the myth that Singapore was impregnable and that the British were invincible, their faith must surely have been severely tested during the incessant bombing and shelling and the resulting devastation of each Japanese air raid. The Japanese bombers carried out their task with destructive frenzy, destroying utilities and killing hapless people with little resistance to repel their incursions. 142 Mackenzie Road, where the Yongs lived and where Elizabeth had set up her marital home was near Government House (now the Istana). The bombing and shelling were unnervingly close; the Japanese aeroplanes came very low, almost to roof level, or so it appeared to the very shaken residents of the area. In fact, there was a direct hit on the kitchen of the Yongs' two-storey terrace house. Despite its proximity to the target of Japanese bombers – presumably Government House – there were endless streams of people seeking shelter with the Yongs, among them, school children. There were also the victims of shelling who straggled past the Yongs' house. Some were too dazed and weary to go any further; the Yongs did what they could in offering them temporary shelter and in giving them hot drinks to fortify them.

By then Elizabeth, who had joined the Medical Auxiliary Services as a volunteer nurse, had seen enough. She was confronted daily with innocent people who got in the way of bombs. The wounds were nightmarish: lost limbs, misplaced guts. When the situation worsened, the casualty centres were closed; those in need of medical help had to go to the General Hospital in Outram Road for treatment. The shelters earmarked for civilians were not bomb-proof; there were cases where those who sought refuge in them were killed when the shelters were hit. The Yongs took the precaution of securing a makeshift shelter of their own with sandbags, but it was not big enough to accommodate all the people staying in the Mackenzie Road house.

There came a day when it was no longer possible to stay there. It was then decided that they themselves should seek shelter elsewhere: York Hill, a government-run centre. But when Elizabeth and her husband, together with her father, stepmother, three sisters, one pregnant sister-in-law and two brothers got there, they were turned away; it was too crowded to take in anymore refugees.

The family was at loss as to where to turn – short of going back to Mackenzie Road – when a cousin of Elizabeth's spotted the anxious group. This cousin was working at the General Hospital in Outram Road. She took the whole family in. That turned out to be the eve of the British surrender.

Saturday, 14 February 1942, was the eve of the Lunar New Year, but instead of the traditional non-stop festive firing of crackers, Singapore was subject to relentless and deafening shelling by the invaders. The next day, 15 February i942, the first day of the Year of the Horse, *The Sunday Times* had just one page. Under the masthead was Governor Sir Shenton Thomas' slogan: "*Singapore must stand; it shall stand*." But before sunset that day, the British had surrendered. The myth of fortress Singapore was shattered irredeemably when the British capitulated. Mercifully, the actual fighting had lasted less than seventy days. It was on the night of 8 December 1941 when the first bombs were dropped on Singapore. In the wee hours of that day, the invaders had landed on the north-east of Peninsular Malaya, at Kota Baru, Kelantan. Then came the sinking of a British battleship, the *Prince of Wales*, and a battle cruiser, the *Repulse*. That took care of British might at sea. Supported by the Imperial Japanese Air Force, the Japanese soldiers charged down the length of the peninsula on bicycles. Only a narrow strait separated the island of Singapore from the southern tip of the peninsula.

On 8 February 1942, the Japanese crossed the damaged but hastily repaired, one-kilometre long causeway that connected the peninsula to the island. Fortified Singapore never did get to test the power and accuracy of its guns. Thought to be strategically located, it turned out that the 46-centimetre cannons were facing the wrong direction. The British military experts were certain that the invaders would come by sea, but the Japanese did not oblige; instead, they came by land. To the populace, the incessant bombing and shelling by the Japanese had been nerve-wracking; to learn of the British surrender and to watch the victorious 25th Army of Japan marching through the streets of Singapore was a nightmare come alive. "We felt the sky had fallen; it seemed like the end of the world," recalled

Mrs Choy. It wasn't quite the end of the world but hell was just around the corner.

Singapore was renamed Syonanto (Syonan for short) by the Japanese, in tribute to their emperor, Hirohito, in the reign of Syowa. (*Nan* literally means south; *to* an island.) The victors from *Dai Nippon* – Mighty Japan – wasted no time in making their presence felt.[1] It soon became alarmingly obvious that they were singling out ethnic Chinese men. The masses were told to report to various police stations taken over by the Japanese. The frightened and confused populace were harangued, given verbal warnings and threats by the Japanese before being sent on their way to register elsewhere. Elizabeth's family first went to a police station in Tanjong Pagar where they were directed to a centre in Jalan Besar. The women of the Yong family were allowed to leave after a night's stay. As they walked out, each was stamped on the arm, to certify that they had been cleared.

It took several days for the men to be processed. It would soon become frighteningly apparent that Chinese men between the ages of fifteen and fifty years were the endangered cohort. But often, it seemed there were no guidelines; much depended on the centre and the officers involved. Apart from age and ethnicity, the hapless person could have been singled out for no other reason than that a particular Japanese officer did not like his looks or manners. Whatever the rules in the selection of the condemned – that was what the massive terrifying exercise amounted to – they were not made known to the masses. As the days went by, the panic intensified, aggravated by dreadful rumours of the detained men being sent away to do forced labour or worse, that they had been summarily executed.

There were gory and macabre details. One version said that the men had been taken to selected spots on the coast where they were ordered to dig a large pit; once the task was completed, they were lined up and shot right there, their bodies falling into their mass grave. Preferred hour: evening. A variation would be that all were shot or bludgeoned or bayonetted to death, their killers not bothering to bury the corpses. Or so the rumours went. They were very close to the truth. In their maniacal, euphemistically labelled 'mopping up', campaign, the Japanese murdered thousands of Chinese civilians – the vast majority were men but there were cases of women and children too – in the span of a fortnight, beginning less than a week after the unconditional surrender of the British. At the end of the war, official estimates placed the total number massacred at five thousand. This has been widely disputed as gross under-estimation.[2]

Elizabeth's father, then in his fifties, was released from the centre. But the Japanese soldiers detained his seventeen-year old son. The last words his father heard before he dragged himself away were the boy's plaintive plea to be allowed to go home. Elizabeth began a desperate search for her brother at the behest of her distraught father, but all she met with during her search were other distressed people, all tearfully and desperately looking for missing members of their families, risking their own lives by going to the centres manned by the Japanese to make futile inquiries. Her father's bewilderment at the disappearance of his favourite child was heart-breaking to Elizabeth. He forgot all about personal safety and wandered aimlessly in the streets, searching. He was close to losing his sanity then. Elizabeth could only conclude that her brother was lost to the family forever.

While the British surrender stunned the masses, people had a way of bouncing back and getting on with living as best they could, no matter how trying the circumstances. With the Japanese came rationing of just about any and everything. (Consequently, a black market in just about any and everything sprung up.) Queuing up for rations became a preoccupation with ordinary folk. The shortage of food worsened as the occupation continued. (Inevitably, inflation soared.) It was just as well that the population could till the land to supplement the meagre rations. Many householders became amateur farmers; manicured gardens were transformed into vegetable beds. Tapioca was the crop of the occupation years. Hens were also kept, for their eggs and their meat; some urban-dwellers even reared pigs within their compounds.

Under the Japanese, the non-Chinese had an easier time; their movements were not restricted, unlike the Chinese. Thus, the Mackenzie Road house had regular visits from two Indian teachers, colleagues of Mrs Choy at St Andrew's. There was also an Indian doctor who visited ever so often. All were there to check whether the Yongs were all right, especially where food was concerned. The Japanese allowed religious practices to continue; services were allowed in churches and there was an order issued that religious buildings must not be used for military purposes.[3] Of the Church of England – Mrs Choy belongs to this – three members of its clergy were allowed the freedom to visit families of their religious affiliation. One of them was none other than the principal of St Andrew's, Canon Adams. It was strictly a matter of permitting the shepherds to tend to their flock. To the pious Yongs, such visits brought them much solace and renewed hope.

The damage inflicted on the Mackenzie Road house was such that anyone could walk in through the back where the kitchen used to be. That was what the Japanese soldiers did as they went on their drunken spree through the town. The first time they came acalling, the menfolk of the family had yet to return from the registration centre. Most of the women were downstairs, petrified at the sudden appearance of the unkempt soldiers in their midst. Before anyone could do anything, one of the soldiers went upstairs and locked himself in the bedroom where Mrs Choy's pregnant sister-in-law Maureen was. The womenfolk could hear Maureen's hysterical shrill pleading. Suddenly, Elizabeth sprang into action. She grabbed a mattress, charged upstairs and banged on the locked door. Her pretext was to return the mattress to the room. That distraction saved her poor sister-in-law from the ordeal that had seemed inevitable. (In the soldier's hasty retreat, he left behind his sword!)

As a result of bomb damage, the Yongs could not secure the house from unwelcome visitors. They – what was left of the family – obtained permission to use a neighbour's garage where the family-members could at least spend nights in relative safety behind a locked door. But there was nothing the Yongs could do about the looting. Practically all the wedding presents from the double wedding were taken.

When it was time, Maureen's baby was born in that badly battered Mackenzie Road house. One of the nurses in the family served as the midwife.[4] It was a twenty-four-hour labour with members of the family anxiously pacing the floor and getting in each other's way. The baby, a bouncing boy, finally came to the world, howling loud enough for the whole neighbourhood to hear. His father, Kon Vui, chose the name Victor for his firstborn.

Soon after the surrender, the Japanese decided to clear the General Hospital in Outram Road and patients were moved to the Mental Hospital way out of town, in Jalan Woodbridge, off Yio Chu Kang Road. This was renamed the Miyako Hospital. Sick internees were also sent there, but the hospital could hardly provide for all the extra patients. Being so far from town, it was difficult to get even basic supplies.

By then, Mrs Choy had ceased to teach or work as a volunteer nurse, and her husband's book-keeping job at Borneo Company no longer existed. Doctors and nurses who knew the couple urged them to set up and run a canteen at Miyako Hospital to provide at least some of the basic goods needed by everyone. The Choys did just that. It certainly was not by design, but before long, the canteen was no longer merely the source of daily essentials. It had evolved into the depository for medicine and food from families of patients in the hospital. Next, it became the effective conduit of messages between the internment camp in Changi and the 'outside' world. The Choys were not about to say no to people who asked for help, especially when it was within their means to do so – passing on some packages and/or messages was definitely within their ability. To them, it was the least they could do to help ease the misery and anxiety of victims of capricious Japanese brutality, to bring a little comfort to the innocent victims of the war. Yes, it was the right thing to do. This led to the arrest of Choy Khun Heng on 29 October 1943 and of his wife, Elizabeth, sixteen days later.

1   To begin with, the victors decreed that Singapore must observe Tokyo time by advancing its clocks by one-and-half hours.

2   See *The Killer They Called A God* by Ian Ward (Media Master, 1993).

3   The enemies' magnanimity towards the church had much to do with a Christian Japanese officer, Lieutenant Andrew Ogawa. See *Priest in Prison* by John Hayter (Graham Brash, Singapore 1991).

4   There was no shortage of nurses among the Yongs. Two of Mrs Choy's sisters, plus several cousins and aunts, were nurses. They continued to work as nurses during the occupation years. Elizabeth's sister Annie was fondly referred to by hospitalised internees as "a ray of sunshine."

VII
LIVING HELL

BY THE TIME of the Choys' arrest, the canteen had moved to the Tan Tock Seng Hospital in Moulmein Road. The directive to clear out of Miyako Hospital came in the wake of the Double Tenth swoop on Changi. Internees in need of medical treatment were housed in hastily-erected huts in Sime Road for greater security, from the Japanese point of view. The strategy was to sever internees' links with the outside world through Miyako Hospital. It was obvious that the Japanese had become suspicious of the contact between civilians and internees at Miyako via the hospital canteen.

Choy Khun Heng was at the Tan Tock Seng Hospital canteen when the Japanese came for him on 29 October 1943. Concern over his non-return mounted as the days went by. Elizabeth was not one to wring her hands and do nothing. Off she went to the Japanese Military Police headquarters and main interrogation and detention centre – number One Orchard Road, the YMCA[1] before the arrival of the Japanese – to ask if she could see her husband. No, she was told. Reluctant to leave the vicinity, she sat on the grass verge across the road directly facing the building, perhaps hoping against hope that her husband might just walk out of the door or that the jailors would relent and allow her to at least see him. There she remained till dusk. It was only when the Japanese police ordered her to leave immediately that she dragged herself away – "with a very heavy heart."

On 15 November 1943, an officer from the *Kempeitai* headquarters turned up at Mackenzie Road and asked if she wanted to see her husband. Of course she did. The man told her that he was there to escort her; he suggested that she bring a blanket in case her husband needed one. (When she went to look for her husband earlier, she had mentioned to the Japanese that her husband had nothing with him, not even a blanket.) The trusting Mrs Choy was relieved that she could at least visit her husband. It turned out to be subterfuge. She was taken to the YMCA. Upon arrival, she was told to remove her watch, her jewellery and to leave her handbag with the duty officers. As Mrs Choy recalls, she reached for a comb in her bag to stick in her hair, but this was taken away from her.

It must have been with a sinking heart that she found herself led to a room – a cell – with at least twenty people in it, prisoners all. The cell was no larger than three by four metres. There was a narrow air vent on one wall. No windows. Hardly any natural light filtered in. The floor was of wooden planks. The inmates sat cross-legged all day long on the floor, facing the corridor, where sentries kept watch round-the-dock.

Separating the inmates from the corridor were ceiling-high iron bars. Towards one end of this wall of bars was a gap for food to be pushed into the cell. Towards the other end was a low gate for prisoners to crawl through. (Doubtless it gave the Japanese victors considerable sadistic pleasure to see the vanquished on all fours.) There was a commode in one corner of the room. To flush, turn on the tap. For washing and drinking, do the same.

This gloomy, damp, filthy and noxious cell was to be Mrs Choy's 'home' for 193 days and nights. Here she was to exist without any change of clothes, any soap to wash, not even a toothbrush or comb to run through her hair. ("I used to love combing my hair.") She was the only female in that cell for most of her incarceration. There was once a Eurasian woman who shared the cell for a few days. It was just as well that Mrs Choy grew up quite free of prudery.

Her cell-mates were a mixed lot: civil servants, doctors, businessmen, young and old, mostly from Singapore (and mostly Chinese) with a few foreigners. They were all victims of the same calamity. There was thus a spirit of camaraderie. Although they were not allowed to talk to each other, someone who knew sign language taught his cell-mates for silent communication. It was really quite easy. The five fingers of the left hand would stand for the vowels: A, E, I, O and U; the thumb is A, the index finger stands for E, the middle finger as I, the ring finger O and the little finger U. The right hand would serve as the marker. For example, if A was the letter wanted, then point to the thumb; all fingers directed at the palm of the other hand would be B, running a finger round the groove between the thumb and the index finger of the other hand would be C... for X, cross the right index finger over the left; for Y, run the index finger downwards, starting from the base of the groove between the thumb and the index finger (or simply follow the life-line in the palm); and for Z, just write the letter in the palm. Certainly not the speediest means of communication, but if there was anything the prisoners had plenty of, it was time.

It was a Mr Dunlop who shared his knowledge of sign language with his fellow inmates. He was quite a sight to behold. There was not a hair on his whole head; not even where eyebrows should be. He was a wonderful cell-mate, doing his utmost to cheer others up. One day, he read Mrs Choy's future. It was a most promising one; he told her that she would be famous, people would read about her in the newspapers. He succeeded in giving her some amusement, his reading being so ludicrous that she could not help but laugh.

Mastery of the sign language helped to distract the prisoners from the pain of maintaining the cross-legged sitting posture for hours on end in that awful cell. And for Mrs Choy, for at least a while, it helped to keep the nagging worries at bay: about her family worrying about her, about the fate of her husband, her missing brother, the mental state of her father, of other family-members in their Mackenzie Road home. Sitting there, there was nothing to look at. There were only the filthy windowless walls and the corridor. Ever so often, the inmates saw other prisoners leaving for, or returning from, interrogation. ("Each time I saw one being taken away for questioning, I would pray that he would come back safe, come back not too badly hurt.") There was a man who did not make it back to his cell; he collapsed and died right there in the corridor after his last session with the *Kempeitai*.

It was almost a relief when it was time to sleep; right on cue, everyone just rolled over and lay there, side by side – like sardines in a can – and tried to seek anaesthesia in sleep. But in that living hell, the *Kempeitai* did not differentiate day from night when it came to interrogation and torture. At night, the screams of the victims of physical abuse would be even more piercing than during the day. There were also occasions when Mrs Choy would be awakened from her fitful sleep by the howling of a colicky baby in the neighbourhood. The crying would not only jerk her out of her sleep but wake her to reality, that she was not in hell. There were nights when hunger spasms would deny her refuge in sleep; to aggravate the situation, she could hear distinctly the itinerant noodle-seller's unmistakable call with his bamboo slabs: "tock tock tock... tock." It was unbearable. She could almost smell the noodles.

Instead of wallowing in self-pity and sorrow, she tried to make life a little better for everyone – at least a little less damp and stinking. The made-in-China woollen blanket that she had brought for her husband came in very useful. This blanket shrank in size as the days went by, as bit by bit was torn off to help plug a leak around the commode. That had to be stealthily done when the sentries were inattentive. But she did ask for, and was given, a stone. She used it to scrub the commode area with all the vigour she could muster; it effectively made the convenience corner somewhat cleaner looking and a lot less smelly. Typically, she would make light of her own plight, feeling instead compassion for her cell-mates, especially the foreigners. "It's not so bad for me because back in North Borneo we were used to it; we didn't have proper facilities there anyway. Even for some households in Singapore in those days, there were no proper toilets. But for the foreigners, it must have been really bad for them, to exist like that in the cell," she grimaced in reminiscence.

A sliver of wood became a much treasured tool. Someone managed to peel a bit off the planks on which they sat. This became a toothpick. It could not have been more treasured if it had been made of precious metal. It was passed round day after day, shared among all the cell-mates to clean their teeth, until there was nothing left.

The prisoners' one consummate obsession was food. This would be pushed into the cell at one end of the wall of bars thrice a day. Each meal was a tiny ball of rice with shreds of vegetables and perhaps bits of what passed as fish or meat. After that came the drink – a bucket of weak tea along with a mug in an indescribable state of filth. The prisoners took turns to drink from the bucket, using that common mug. As Mrs Choy wryly recalled: "When a person was newly incarcerated and once the initial shock of imprisonment had subsided, he or she could be philosophical and daydream of the 'ideal' world of peace and harmony. One would even be all-wise and come up with solutions to attain Utopia. But alas, reality soon gripped the prisoner as hunger pangs demanded satisfaction. By then it would be nigh impossible to think constructively."

Food, or the lack of it, was foremost on the prisoner's mind. It was sheer agony, lying there on the hard floor, breathing in the suffocating and nauseating stench of the cell and of all the unwashed cell-mates, unable to shut out the ugly and terrifying reality around by going to sleep. If the physical abuse did not kill her first, she was convinced that she would simply die of hunger. She vowed that if she survived the war, she would never overeat, in sympathy with the countless millions in the world who had to live with hunger all their lives.

The prisoners unashamedly begged for food. One obvious source came from new cell-mates. The new prisoners would invariably be too distraught to eat on the first day. The others did not need any invitation to scrape up what was left uneaten. However, for those on a starvation diet for a prolonged period, there might come a time when the hunger pangs would no longer bother them, or they would no longer feel them. At least that was the case with Mrs Choy. There came a stage during her incarceration when she no longer felt hungry; she had no appetite for food and no desire to eat. A few weeks before her discharge – she, of course, had no idea that she would be released – her portion of food was in fact increased. But she just could not eat it and gave it to her fellow inmates.

Despite the appalling state of the prisoners' existence, at least some retained their sense of humour, or common sense. There were those who complained of constipation. No bowel movement for seven days, one groaned. They asked their jailors for laxatives. One detainee, a Malay, knew better. He pointed out the obvious: "How can there be anything to pass out when you haven't any food in your stomach?"

But the prisoners' complaints of constipation did get them some response. The jailors decided some physical movement should fix the problem. There would thus be daily rounds of exercise. The prisoners were not let out of their cells; they had to exercise right where they were. Each cell had a leader and Mrs Choy was appointed the leader of her cell: "Probably because everyone knew I was a school teacher." There would be first some limb stretching, followed by running round the cell until the sentries said "stop." The sentries were quite mad, or possibly plain sadistic. On some days, the prisoners would be kept running round and round and round the crammed cell for perhaps an hour. But no matter; to Mrs Choy, it was infinitely better than sitting on the floor.[2] Standing up gave the prisoners a peek of the world outside through the narrow air vent on one wall. Mrs Choy recalls glimpses of cyclists in the streets. "It seemed so strange out there; so bright, so few people, a different world." The whole scene was rather surreal but the ugly reality was right there, with the bug bites to wake the daydreamers.

The exercise sessions gave the prisoners the chance to get rid of some of those awful bugs. They were all over the cell and all over the inmates. For the bugs at least, it must have been a marvellous existence, feasting to their fill on all those captive bodies. While the inmates moved mindlessly round like zombies, they would pick off as many of the bugs clinging on them as they could. Mrs Choy would also be snuffing the life out of the colonies of bugs on the walls as she went round the cell. On some nights, she just could not sleep with all the bugs attacking her with such vicious abandon. She retaliated by exterminating them; she reckons that she was responsible for the deaths of several thousand bugs in the cell.

In that living hell, a source of comfort to Mrs Choy came from the presence of the Anglican Bishop of Singapore, John Leonard Wilson.[3] He was in the cell next to where Mrs Choy was. When he took the drill, instead of leading the motley group through their paces by shouting "*ichi, ni, san, shi*" – Japanese for one, two, three, four – the Bishop would be spiritedly hollering: "Be of good cheer; lift up your hearts" loud enough for his voice to be heard beyond his cell. To Mrs Choy who never for a moment lost faith, to hear his voice in that living hell was a source of immense comfort.

There came a very special day for Mrs Choy during her incarceration. A visiting Japanese senior military officer noticed the squalid condition of the prison, including the corridors and expressed his annoyance at the unsanitary state of the place. The resourceful Mrs Choy volunteered to scrub the corridors. She would do almost anything to be able to straighten her knees and change her posture. To her, the long hours of inactivity, sitting on the hard floor of that dank cell was a very effective form of torture: "truly unbearable." It would have been far more sufferable if she had been assigned to do hard labour. That day, she was given permission to scrub the corridors. When she reached the cell where Bishop Wilson was – when the sentry was not watching – Mrs Choy knelt to receive holy communion. The Bishop consecrated some rice, stale and somewhat burnt, and for wine, water from the commode. To Mrs Choy, that simple act recharged her spiritually, it reinforced her with immeasurable fortitude, enabling her to withstand abuse and torture with dignity. To reward her for the hard work scrubbing the floor, she was given a double portion of food that day. But to her, she had already been amply rewarded. She blissfully offered the extra portion of food to her cell-mates.

Elizabeth Choy Su-Moi was never charged for any specific crime. The *Kempeitai* wanted information out of her – and from her husband. She could only guess that her detention, her husband's too, had to do with the destruction of ships in the Singapore harbour in September 1943. (By the time of her arrest, she had learnt of the success of Operation Jaywick.) In retrospect, it appeared that the *Kempeitai* was particularly incensed by evidence of money having been smuggled into Changi. The Choys were indeed guilty of having had an active role in that (and radio parts). In fact, it was Bishop Wilson who had started the flow of money into Changi before his own internment in March 1943 and had arranged for the flow to continue when he was interned. The money was needed for a camp fund, for the specific purpose of buying desperately-needed medicine and additional food for the internees. The *modus operandi* was this: the Bishop's secretary would bring the money (usually $10,000 a time) to the Choys at Miyako and the Choys would forward it to Changi as and when trusted internees visited the hospital. The money would be carefully hidden, for example, in cigarette cartons (the Japanese sentries were not bothered by internees buying cigarettes through intermediaries from outside of camp) or water pipes needed for repairs. During the *Kempeitai*'s search of Changi, the camp fund was discovered. To them, there could only be one use for the money – for espionage and other anti-Japanese activities.

Typically, on looking back years later, instead of indignation and anger, Mrs Choy was bemused, and almost amused, that the Japanese could ever suspect her and her husband of espionage; she rationalised that the Japanese were in fact paying them a compliment. When the British returned in 1945, she was given the opportunity to wreak vengeance against her erstwhile jailors. She was asked: "Who would you want to have executed?" She would not give a single name. She told the British: "It's all over, finished. I don't blame the soldiers; it was the war that was wicked and evil. The soldiers had to serve their country, to carry out their duty. I shall not forget; but I shall forgive."

There were about six Japanese officers who took turns to interrogate Elizabeth Choy Su-Moi. All could speak English. It was thus mostly just one interrogator present at any one time. The Japanese officers were not about to accept a denial or a plea of ignorance. The fact that she was a woman was irrelevant to them. Initially, the interrogation was done daily. It could take place any time of the day or night. Later, there might be a week's break in between. She was questioned, cajoled, harangued, threatened, slapped, kicked and beaten. The interrogators' favourite practice was to alternate between being civil and being beastly. Of the officers involved, the one who left the sharpest impact on her memory was probably *Kempeitai* Warrant Officer Monai Tadamori, who was about the same age as Mrs Choy. He could be quite charming and jovial when he chose to. But one day, he suddenly punched Mrs Choy. "He did it out of the blue. I got very angry. It was the one time that I got so angry that I would have killed him if I could." For the rest of that session, she refused to utter a single word.

A common tactic adopted by the interrogators would be to switch from one topic to another. But they consistently wanted her to confess to being anti-Japanese and pro-British and to give the names of others who were anti-Japanese and pro-British. She denied being either anti- or pro- anyone. No number of slaps would make her change her answer, that she was neither but that she would help anyone in need. For good measure, she told her interrogators that if she found them in need of help, she would be just as unhesitant in doing what she could for them. They tried to get answers from her on subjects that she was totally ignorant of. For example: she was asked where a particular British banker was and where he had hidden the bank's money. Days before the British capitulated, 'everyone' seemed to have heard of the frantic burning of papers at a bank. She hadn't the foggiest idea whether the bank had burnt documents or paper currency and she certainly did not know where the banker was. She told her interrogators what she had heard, no more, no less. But the question was asked repeatedly.

In one session, the interrogator's method changed. Instead of demanding names from her, she was given names. Her interrogator called out names and asked if she knew any of them. To each she answered yes, because it was the truth – she did know the person. When the interrogator was through with the list, he rather smugly informed her that the people named were all in the same detention centre as she was. He wanted to know her relationship with everyone of them. She told the Japanese that she helped them when they asked for help, supplying them with biscuits or other food items or toiletries or medicine. She asked her interrogator why he had not asked her if she knew these people earlier on, for it dawned on her that that was what the Japanese wanted out of her. She reiterated that it did not make her anti-Japanese because she had helped people in need. The Japanese had separately checked and grilled many people and these people had unanimously spoken of Mrs Choy's kind-heartedness. This her interrogators told her, and yet they still would not release her.

There were the occasions when she was stripped to the waist, forced to kneel and hold a chair over her head. For good measure, she was given the electric shock treatment. This was on 8 December 1943 when she was subjected to a long session of interrogation by Warrant Officer Monai Tadamori.[4] Since slapping, hitting and yelling at her did not get him the answers he wanted, he had her kneel on a sharp-edged plank, immobilised her by tying her to a wooden rack and gave her the electric shock treatment. It was to leave her with a life-long fear of electricity.[5] Like extreme hunger, Mrs Choy could find no words to adequately describe the pain that went through her whole being during the experience.

During the torture, it was impossible to show defiance and be brave; it was impossible to suppress the screams, or to stop the tears and mucus from streaming down her face. It seemed like the electrocution was going on forever. When the current was finally switched off, the interrogation would continue. Still she did not confess. To Mrs Choy, she could not confess to something she knew was untrue. It would implicate others. It was just not right and she could not do it. Not even if it meant more physical abuse at the hands of her bestial jailors.

The Japanese made one more try. This time, they threw in psychological pressure. It took place the very next day, on 9 December 1943. Mrs Choy was once again taken for questioning and again she did not give the Japanese the answers they sought. She was tied up again on a rack, kneeling on the sharp edge of a plank. She was told that since she wanted to see her husband, they were going to grant her just that. Choy Khun Heng was brought in and made to kneel beside his wife. That was the first time she set eyes on him since his arrest six weeks earlier. He too was tied to a wooden frame. The two were questioned together. Since neither one gave satisfactory answers, Mrs Choy was again given the electric shock punishment. In later testimony given by her husband, the electric shock torture lasted some fifteen minutes; the intense pain caused Mrs Choy to yell uncontrollably. But at the end of it, she still refused to 'confess'.

Perhaps in a final attempt at pushing the Choys over the edge into confessing, their jailors sentenced them to death. Mrs Choy was to be taken to Johor; she would be beheaded at eight o'clock the next morning while her husband's head would roll two hours later. The tormentors told the Choys to say goodbye to each other. The Choys did, with tears and bursting hearts, as Mrs Choy painfully recalled. "If we were executed, we die for the truth; it would be an honourable death."

When Choy Khun Heng was arrested on 29 October 1943, he was accused of assisting espionage, sending wireless sets to the internment camp and money to the internees.[6] He was first taken to the YMCA in Orchard Road; an hour later, he was transferred to the Central Police Station. But it was back again to the YMCA where he was kept for twenty days – starting early November 1943. Here he was questioned, kicked, beaten and burnt by officers of the *Kempeitai* as well as by the interpreters. (Unlike the officers who interrogated his wife, those who interrogated him had interpreters present.) He was made to kneel on a rough plank with a triangular iron bar between his knees. Ever so often, one of the Japanese would viciously stamp on the bar. His tormentors also used iron rods, bamboo sticks and ropes to beat him up. Cigarettes were used to burn him. Then there was the water treatment. He was pushed into a tub of water, forcing him to take in water until he was all bloated and semi-conscious. His tormentors would then lay him on the floor and jump on his abdomen. He too was put through the electric shock treatment. He was made to kneel with his hands and legs tied. Two leads from a generator were applied to his body and legs. Then there was the agony of seeing his wife being tortured and hearing the sentence meted out to them.

He was in the Central Police Station for three months. Here the detainees were fed twice a day; each meal a handful of rice with dribbles of starchy gravy and a little pepper. At one stage, he became so ill that his jailors sent him to Miyako Hospital (where he had operated the canteen) for treatment. He was there for three months. "When he was discharged, it was back to the YMCA before being transferred to the military prison. He was 'tried' on 25 May 1944 and sentenced to twelve years of rigorous imprisonment. On the very next day, Mrs Choy was released. She walked out of One Orchard Road in the same clothes she wore when she walked in 193 days before.[7] She did not know if her husband was dead or alive.

Throughout her ordeal, Mrs Choy's strength of character was there for all to see. Even the Japanese showed their admiration, albeit reluctantly. No matter how hard they tried, by words or by blows, they failed to squeeze the 'confession' they wanted from her. In defeat, they conceded that dealing with her was like dealing with officials of Scotland Yard. Presumably, that was a compliment. After each session, no matter how severe the beating she had just had, she would walk back to her cell as resolutely as when she walked out. Even after the electric shock torture, she managed to return to the cell on her own. (The exception was after she was tortured in the presence of her husband. She tried to walk unaided back, but fainted before she could reach her cell.) Her cell-mates could not but notice that she was a plucky woman. Whatever the pain that wracked her body, whatever turmoil she was going through mentally, she kept these very well hidden. Typically, she was far more concerned about the agony of others. She prayed constantly; she hung on to her abiding faith. Above all, she was thankful that her mother had died before calamity befell her family and was thus spared the mental anguish of a parent whose children were at the mercy of a merciless enemy.

Mrs Choy had personally witnessed the brutality inflicted by the *Kempeitai* on many fellow prisoners. Bishop Wilson was whipped with wet, knotted ropes; his body was swollen, his bruises turned him a ghoulish blue-black and he could barely walk.[8] Robert Heeley Scott, head of the Far East Bureau of the British Ministry of Information was seen being led down a corridor of the YMCA after interrogation; his face puffy, his body misshapen.[9] A cell-mate was going stark crazy. His children happened to be pupils of St Andrew's School where Mrs Choy had taught. He was the victim of typical psychological trickery. He had been told that his wife and sons were to be beheaded. After hours of persuasion, Mrs Choy succeeded in convincing him that it was all a bluff on the part of the Japanese.

Her own misfortune obviously had not diminished her store of compassion. She felt sorry for the man who was a *towkay*, one of standing in the business community, a person who lived in a luxurious mansion and used to be driven by chauffeurs in fancy cars. To be reduced to sharing a cell with over twenty others, living on a starvation diet must have been, as Mrs Choy saw it, the greatest torture and humiliation of his life. For her tormentors, she tried to find reason for their bestiality. On the one hand, it was truly beyond her comprehension how anyone could inflict such cruelty and brutality on another human being as the *Kempeitai* did; on the other hand, she believed, she wanted to believe, that in their hearts they were not really so nefarious and inhuman. She wanted very much to believe that it was their military obligations that made them so abjectly abominable.

Mrs Choy was in a daze when she went home on 26 May 1944. Yet, she suspected that she might be under observation by the

Kempeitai and did not want to endanger anyone by talking to people on the street. In any case, people kept away, especially those who knew she had a husband still under detention. For all they knew, she might have made a deal with the Japanese; she might have been released to obtain information or to entrap others. She was sensitive to their fears and kept to herself. It was just as well that she found a job in the restaurant of a sailors' association that provided living quarters for the staff. Her job as a cashier in the restaurant earned her $80 a month.[10]

The Japanese seemed to fall as speedily as they conquered. When they surrendered on 14 August 1945, the British were not ready to officially accept the capitulation! An amphibious invasion of Malaya was being assembled in India at that time; another three weeks went by before they finally arrived as the 'victors'. It would take yet another ten days or so before the British Military Administration could set up some semblance of control on the land they had abandoned in 1942. The formal date of Japanese capitulation: 12 September 1945.

During the occupation years, news was a rare commodity; mostly, just rumours. Rumours were flying in the weeks before August 1945 that the Japanese were about to surrender. No one dared to openly talk about it. Mrs Choy's father and some other members of the Yong family were in Endau, Johor.[11] It happened that Mrs Choy's stepmother had become pregnant there. As Endau had no medical facilities, the Japanese allowed the expectant mother to rush to Singapore in a goods lorry. Her baby girl, named Judith, was delivered by Caesarian section – using just local anaesthetics – by Dr Benjamin H. Sheares[12] at the Kandang Kerbau Maternity Hospital.

As rumours of the Japanese surrender became more and more rife, family-members in Singapore thought of a means of getting a message to Endau. It was a cautious and innocuously worded one, hoping Elizabeth's father could read between the lines. The message suggested that he and the other family-members with him might like to get permission to visit Singapore to see his daughter, born on the last day of July 1945 and to attend the wedding anniversary of his son Kon Vui which fell on 16 August. The father understood. Thus, he had returned to Singapore with a stepsister when Japanese capitulation became real news. It was only then that Elizabeth could openly look for her husband. She traced him to a prison in Outram Road. There she went, in the company of a British soldier, to free him. By then, Choy Khun Heng had been a prisoner for nearly two years.

When the war ended, three members of the Yong family had perished: A brother, a cousin and an uncle. Choy Khun Heng regained his freedom, but he never fully regained his health.

---

1   Headquartered in Geneva, Switzerland, since 1878, the Christian movement took root in Singapore in 1903. It acquired the Orchard Road site on a 999-year lease in 1904. A three-storey mock Tudor structure was built. This was the building the Japanese used. The YMCA's billiard room was transformed beyond recognition into prison cells.

2   Not all prisoners shared Mrs Choy's enthusiasm. There were those who could barely stand as a result of the torture meted out to them by the jailors.

3   The Bishop was earlier interned at the Changi Prison; in the aftermath of Double Tenth, he was among the internees identified by the *Kempeitai* for interrogation. He was first sent to another makeshift detention centre in Smith Street before being moved to the YMCA.

4   At the war crimes trial in Singapore after the Second World War, he was sentenced to death by hanging.

5   Her paranoia is such that she dreaded all electrical appliances; even the simple act of touching a switch was studiously avoided.

6   He recounted his imprisonment by the *Kempeitai* and the punishment meted out to him and fellow detainees during the trial of twenty-one members of the *Kempeitai*, conducted by the British War Crimes Court in 1946 in Singapore. The *Kempeitai* members were charged with the arrest, ill-treatment and torture of fifty-seven civilians and inmates of Changi Prison; fifteen had died at their hands. When the trial took place in March 1946, Mrs Choy had left for Britain. Her affidavit was presented as evidence.

7   These are now with the National Museum of Singapore.

8   The *Kempeitai* tortured him on three consecutive days. See *Priest in Prison* by John Hayter (Graham Brash, 1991).

9   Scott, like Bishop Wilson, had been a Changi Prison internee. The *Kempeitai* had identified him as a prime suspect; they were convinced that Scott was behind the destruction of ships in the Singapore harbour. Both Scott and the Bishop survived their ordeals. Bishop Wilson later told Mrs Choy that a source of immense joy to him during those dark days was the singing of the golden oriole which he could hear when he put his ear against the cracks in the wall that separated the inmates from the outside world.

10 The Japanese issued their own currency, the 'banana notes', to replace Straits currency, 'tiger notes', at par. During the occupation, the value of banana notes eroded rapidly. Towards the last few months of the occupation, $80 could at best pay for a tin of sardines on the black market. By the end of the war, the notes were totally worthless.

11 Her father was among the Chinese rounded up the Japanese and sent to a deletion camp about 200 kilometres from Singapore along the east coast of the peninsula: Endau, renamed New Syonan. Sending civilian population out of Singapore was the Japanese solution to the severe food shortage that came with the occupation. (The Eurasians and those of the Roman Catholic faith were dispatched to Bahau, renamed Fuji Village, in Negri Sembilan, on the west coast of the peninsula.)

12 From 1970 to 1981, President of Singapore; the Republic's second Head of State.

VIII

IT'S A WONDERFUL WORLD

TO LONDON – to see the Queen! Mrs Elizabeth Choy was dressed in a beautifully tailored *qipao*[1] which showed off her slimness and height to perfection. That *qipao* was part of her wedding trousseau. Strangely, the looters who ransacked her Mackenzie Road home repeatedly during the Japanese occupation were not interested in her clothes. The material of this *qipao* was of fine silk; flowers in full bloom in variegated pink and white, interspersed with leaf patterns in lime green, against a background of deep purplish-blue; the piping was in a matching shade of pink; to complete the outfit, intricate traditional hand-made frog-buttons of the same material as the piping. To Elizabeth, her dressing would not be complete without a flower in her hair. But that summer morning, there were no fresh bloom available to her! She improvised and used a twig of bamboo-like leaves instead; this twig enchantingly echoed the green hue of the leaf patterns on her garment. She was indeed the picture of oriental grace as she waited for her audience with Queen Elizabeth (the past Queen Mother).

It was an experience Elizabeth Choy Su-Moi never forgot. There she was, as she related, an "almost wild woman from Borneo," walking into Buckingham Palace, escorted by Sir Shenton Thomas and Lady Thomas[2] who, the press noted, had cut short their vacation so that they could personally escort her to the Palace. It was the Queen who had asked to have a private chat with Mrs Choy, who had arrived in Britain in the early wintry months of 1946.

When the invitation from Buckingham Palace came, Elizabeth was still on cloud nine, having witnessed the official victory celebrations of 8 June. There was the magic and pageantry of the parade. Then there was the royal garden party. Each and everyone seemed bursting with joy and goodwill. She met guests from all parts of the world and renewed friendships with people she had met under vastly different circumstances. There were familiar faces, faces of former detainees. There, at the party, she met Admiral Lord Louis Mountbatten and Lady Mountbatten again. Admiral Mountbatten was the Supreme Allied Commander who went to Singapore to accept the formal surrender of the Japanese. It was Lady Mountbatten, who had heard through the Red Cross of Mrs Choy's work as a member of the Medical Auxiliary Services during the months before the fall of Singapore and of the suffering she and her husband had been through as prisoners, who arranged for Mrs Choy and her husband to witness the ceremony at City Hall (then still known as the Municipal Building) back in Singapore.

Mrs Choy had also been invited to a garden party at Government House where Admiral Mountbatten was the guest-of-honour. Other guests at the party could not but notice that the Admiral was at Mrs Choy's side for most of the time. (Later, Mrs Choy was teased for monopolising the Supreme Commander. It appeared that Admiral Mountbatten was keenly interested in Mrs Choy's personal account of life as a prisoner of the Japanese occupation forces.) Mrs Choy was also invited to visit some internment camps in Jakarta, Indonesia. A highlight of her Indonesian visit was her chance meeting with Sukarno, the Indonesian nationalist who had proclaimed Indonesia's independence on 17 August 1945.

The unexpected happened when Mrs Choy met the Queen. The normally down-to-earth Elizabeth was so looking forward to the occasion, so excited and thrilled at the prospect of meeting not just a member of the British royalty but the Queen herself that she could not sleep a wink the night before. When she was finally presented to the Queen, she was so overcome by the occasion and the graciousness of Her Majesty that she broke down and cried. The audience lasted perhaps half an hour. Not having outgrown her schoolgirlish penchant for autographs, Elizabeth had, before the meeting, consulted Sir Shenton on the propriety of asking the Queen for one. The Englishman was bemused and advised against it. Mrs Choy accepted his word and refrained from asking. It was, however, quite proper to present a little gift to the Queen. This she remembered to do. Four days after that unforgettable occasion – 25 July 1946 – there was a very pleasant surprise for her. A parcel arrived; it was from the Palace. In it, a signed portrait of the Queen! There was also a letter penned by the lady-in-waiting in courtly style, expressing the Queen's enjoyment of Mrs Choy's visit:

> *The Queen now commands me to write and say that Her Majesty is causing this signed photograph to be sent to you, as the Queen would like you to have it. I am to say that Her Majesty was so pleased to see you on Wednesday of this week, and the Queen does indeed appreciate the little token of jade which you so kindly brought for Her Majesty's gracious acceptance.*

Mrs Choy's world had taken a 180-degree turn. The war was over and she was a celebrity, a war heroine. Word spread quickly about the brave and admirable woman-detainee who defied the *Kempeitai* and did not kowtow to all the threats, bullying and torture meted out to her. She was probably the longest incarcerated Asian female civilian in Singapore,[3] and she and her husband were the only couple to be arrested and imprisoned by the Japanese. The fact that she was fluent in the English language and could thus easily field questions certainly enhanced her attractiveness to foreign correspondents. It was hardly surprising that media correspondents thirsty for news and real-life stories would seek her out for interviews.

The Red Cross offered the Choys a trip to Britain to help them forget the brutality and cruelty they had suffered at the hands of the *Kempeitai* and to recuperate. But there was so much for the Choys to do, to pick up their shattered lives again. The house they lived in had been badly damaged and looted. Urgent repair work needed to be done for it to be a home again. There was the necessity of returning to work too. And Mr Choy did not like to travel. So Mrs Choy went alone that January day of 1946, taking her very first aeroplane trip in a military aircraft. There were several stops on the way for refuelling. By the time the plane landed in Cairo, Egypt, the weather had become uncomfortably chilly. Mrs Choy had gone unprepared for the temperate zone and it was winter! The Red Cross came to her rescue and provided her with clothes adequate for the biting cold. Some of the garments were obviously meant for men but that did not bother her. She was grateful to have them. It was planned that she would stay in Britain for six months. In the end, she stayed for all of four years.

Mrs Choy had definitely not lost her zest for life, nor her eagerness to help others. It did not take long for her to regain her robust health. Despite the starvation diet during her incarceration, the appallingly unhygienic environment, the physical abuse and mental anguish she had gone through, she was nevertheless in amazingly good health. She did not even have skin infections – scabies, for example – as most prisoners did. Yet, when she stepped out of One Orchard Road in May 1944, she was a walking skeleton with a waspwaist which her two hands could easily encircle. But all she needed was proper food to put back some flesh on her. Weight aside, she had also lost quite a lot of hair. During her incarceration, in lieu of a comb, she ran her fingers through her locks and when she did, found clumps of hair in her hand. That loss, too, was easily arrested and reversed with proper diet.

Much of her time during her first year in Britain was spent travelling: sightseeing, renewing friendships and meeting people. Among those she visited was a pen-pal of long standing. In the mid-1920s, when she was still in her native North Borneo, she and an English girl, Stella, had started to write to each other. Over the years, the two girls kept up the correspondence. After twenty years and a world war, the pen-pals finally met. By then, Stella was Mrs Cloon. No sooner had they met, Stella's pen-pal from the Orient moved in as a baby-sitter for two weeks! It came about because Stella and her husband – the latter having just returned from the army – wanted to go away for a short holiday. But there were their young children to worry about. The moment Mrs Choy learnt of their predicament, she volunteered to help. It did not occur to her that it could have been problematic for her, not knowing the English way of life. She only realised it after her good deed was done.

Just a few days after Mrs Choy's visit to Buckingham Palace to meet the Queen, she received a telephone call from someone identifying himself as E. N. T. Cummings. The caller informed her that she was to go with him to Buckingham Palace on 30 July 1946, to meet Princess Elizabeth (now Queen Elizabeth II).[4] Mrs Choy's immediate reaction was to ask him: "Are you drunk?" He was very sober and serious. It seemed that the Princess had heard much about the courage and devotion of the nurses of Singapore. Mrs Choy, who had served as a volunteer nurse in the Medical Auxiliary Services, was chosen to represent the nursing corps. Mr Cummings, Mrs Choy soon learnt, was to represent former internees of the Changi internment camp. For the meeting, she chose another *qipao* from her wedding trousseau. This too was of fine silk; the floral design was in vibrant shades of pink and tangerine on a background of midnight blue; the piping was of satin, in pink. The finishing touch – a pink carnation in her hair.

Mr Cummings and Mrs Choy were to jointly present Princess Elizabeth with a very special silver casket of the finest Kelantanese craftsmanship of Malaya. It was an heirloom belonging to an internee who had kept it buried for safekeeping during the occupation. Separately, buried in the grounds of Changi Prison internment camp, was a bottle which contained a list of 605 names and addresses of civilian internees. This was their pledge to repay a debt of gratitude to the 125 nurses who had taken care of them. After the war, the bottle was unearthed and the list retrieved. Mr

Cummings told the British media in 1946 that "no human being could forget what those nurses meant to us." Mrs Choy was one of those nurses. A scroll recording the courageous deeds of the nurses during those terrifying days was placed in the silver casket and presented to the future queen.

At every opportunity during her four-year sojourn in Britain, Mrs Choy went in search of new experiences, sights and sounds. She took part in fruit-picking in East Anglia, camping in the orchards during harvest season. She cycled to see places she had only heard of or read about. Back in the interior of North Borneo, fishing had been one of her favourite pastimes. Now in Britain, she eagerly tried trout fishing in the rivers of Yorkshire Dales. She made a point of visiting Loch Lomond, Scotland's largest lake. To get there, she took a train to Gairlochhead, then walked the rest of the way, eagerly. And there before her was the magnificent lake; the sight was breathtaking, with distant majestic glaciated mountains highlighting its shimmering surface, fringed by verdant woods. As she stood there, Mrs Choy said a silent 'thank you' – for she was there to pay personal homage to Loch Lomond. "While in prison with no future before her, the tune of the popular English song in praise of the lake kept coming to her head. It helped her through those dreadfully empty days.

Mrs Choy also visited other European countries: France, the Netherlands and Switzerland. Each stop was an intoxicating experience for her. During her four years away from her tropical home, she experienced both the best of an English summer and the worst of its winter. There was the winter of 1946-47 when she went to Swaledale and stood on the highest moor she could find. The whiteness was dazzling; it was bleak and at the same time, awesome. And of course it was very cold. She thought about the extreme hunger she had lived through. She concluded that it is as impossible to use words to convey the meaning of 'cold' as it is with 'hunger'.

Her first year in Britain was mostly to recuperate, to forget and to sightsee. In her second year away from home, she pursued a domestic science course at the Northern Polytechnic. It was to her yet another year well spent; in the process, enhancing her understanding of the English and their way of life. Then it was back to familiar territory, teaching. In her third year in Britain, she taught in a London County primary school. It was a thoroughly enjoyable time teaching the children and making friends with the other teachers. She was the only ethnic Chinese on the staff of some twenty teachers. If there was any racial discrimination, she was spared as she encountered none. In her fourth year, it was art appreciation.

Mrs Choy did it in a rather odd and roundabout manner. She became a model. Costs aside, there were limited vacancies for art students and she felt it would not be fair to deprive a younger person of a place. (By then, she was in her late-thirties.) But she did not want to miss the opportunity to acquire a greater appreciation of the fine arts. She discovered that there was a demand for models; so she became one, often posing in the nude. Her logic: she could pick up pointers from the artists (for free) while working as a model (for which she was of course paid). As a child of the wild tropical east growing up in the company of the Kadazans and other natives of the land, nudity had been very much part of the landscape. She was perfectly at ease posing in her birthday suit for classes – very solemn atmosphere, she recalls – in several art schools in London.

Narcissism was certainly not a characteristic associated with Mrs Choy, but she soon found that her body – her form – was the object of much artistic appreciation in the art circle of London. For one brought up in a traditional, conservative Chinese family, her Christian piety strengthened through years of exposure to the teachings of missionaries, the artistic world or perspective must surely have been quite a revelation to her. Her feet, for example. They never interested her; to her, her size-seven feet had always seemed rather large and ungainly. But not so to the artists. It was probably Jacob Epstein the sculptor who first commented on her "beautiful feet." They were seen as quite perfect, with just the right curvature and instep. ("Must be from running barefoot and climbing all those trees in the jungles of Borneo," chuckled Mrs Choy in recollection.)

Sculptors were raving about her high cheek bones too. Then there was her spine. There was much appreciation of the allure of its straightness. One photographer wanted to capture just her spine on film. Others – photographers, oil painters and sculptors – wanted the whole form, as well as head-and-shoulder presentation of the model. One woman sculptor she posed for was Dora Gordine.[5] Two statuettes of Mrs Choy were done, one called Serene Jade, the other Flawless Crystal. Gordine made six bronze copies of each. Mrs Choy liked Serene Jade so much that she bought one from the sculptress, numbered one of six. A third sculpture had been started, but by then, Mrs Choy felt she should be home in Singapore.

If it were left to her, she would probably have stayed on indefinitely. In Britain, she felt free; truly able to forget the trauma of the Japanese occupation and what she had been through. But her sense of responsibility prevailed when she learnt of her youngest sister Marie's lack of interest in pursuing further studies or a career after sitting for the school leaving examinations. Eldest sister Elizabeth had been surrogate mother for most of Marie's life, until her detention by the Japanese and later, her extended stay in Britain. Now she felt guilty that she had neglected her baby sister. She knew where her duty lay, and sailed for home on board the *Andre Laban*. It was 23 December 1949 when the ship docked in Singapore.[6]

In less than four years, Mrs Choy was back in London to attend the Coronation, on 2 June 1953, of the Princess she had met. Mrs Choy was quite a sensation during her five-week stay. The city was of course chock-full of celebrities gathered for the Coronation, but the press nevertheless noticed the oriental woman, what with her wardrobe of form-fitting *qipao* and the flower in her hair that had by then become very much her signature style. The *qipao* underscored her Chinese ethnicity; the flower reflected a life-long love of nature, of the ways of the Kadazans of the Land Below the Wind. For the Coronation, she had a very special *qipao*[7] tailored by the famed Shanghainese *qipao* specialist See Kwei Sung of Orchard Road; it had cost her a princely sum of $130. It was of satin material, in off-white, hand embroidered with a dragon motif; the special touch

TOP From left: Su-Yung, Kon Vui and Su-Moi, Tenom, British North Borneo, circa 1915.

BOTTOM Family portrait, 1930s. Back row, from left: Elizabeth's aunts Jessie and Doreen and Elizabeth. Front row, from left: Elizabeth's cousin Pung Onn Fah, his mother Yong Lan Jing, Elizabeth's mother Wong Pui Chin, Elizabeth's cousin and her daughter, and Elizabeth's aunt Elsie.

ABOVE Elizabeth, circa 1930, thrilled to attend the Convent of the Holy Infant Jesus in Singapore.

LEFT Elizabeth in 1933.

TOP RIGHT 'Then we were six.' Back row from left to right: Annie Su-Ni, Kon Vui, Doris Su-Yung and Chau Vui. Marie Su-Tshin seated with Elizabeth Su-Moi in front.

BOTTOM RIGHT Elizabeth with her sister Marie, circa 1935.

FAR LEFT   Elizabeth before her
marriage, circa 1941.

ABOVE   Elizabeth (left) and her
aunt, Jessie (right), with a friend.
Both Elizabeth and Jessie were
born in 1910.

LEFT   Elizabeth at a class picnic at
Pulau Ubin, 1937.

LEFT   Portrait of the newly-wedded Choys, 16 August 1941.

ABOVE   Mrs Choy, sporting a scarf, on her honeymoon with her husband, Khun Heng, in dark-coloured shirt, and members of their family, 1941.

ABOVE Legislative Counsellor, 1951.

TOP LEFT Portrait of Mrs Choy wearing her OBE medal.

BOTTOM LEFT Mrs Choy receiving the St. Andrew's School long-service award from Mrs Sorby Adams, 1950.

LEFT   Mrs Choy wearing her coronation *qipao* embroidered with the Chinese couplet: 'Long live the Queen; may there be universal peace'.

ABOVE   Mrs Choy appearing on BBC television, 1953.

RIGHT   Mrs Choy's first taste of a doughnut, accompanied by a cup of coffee, during her lecture tour in North America, 1954.

ABOVE   Mrs Choy with US Vice
President Richard Nixon and
Mrs Nixon in Washington during
Mrs Choy's lecture tour to North
America in 1954.

RIGHT   Mrs Choy showing
a Malayan sarong in Ottawa during
her North American lecture tour,
1954.

RIGHT The Choys at an
official reception in honour
of the Duchess of Kent, 1954.

LEFT Elizabeth with her daughters (from left) Lynette, Irene and Bridget, 1955.

ABOVE Mrs Choy playing the part of a mother in a skit performed at the YWCA, circa 1954.

ABOVE Proud parents on Bridget's
ninth birthday, 1959, with Lynette
on the left and Irene to the right.

was the eight-word couplet in Chinese: "Long live the Queen; may there be universal peace."

The historic occasion was, for Mrs Choy, marred by an embarrassing incident: she got drunk at the Coronation banquet. It was the first time she tasted champagne, and the effect on her was far from bubbly. Mrs Choy had always believed that she could eat and drink anything, hot or cold, cooked or raw, without suffering any uncomfortable side effects. (Her family-members attest to that; she is known as the woman with the stomach of a horse.) Well, perhaps almost anything. She became quite sick there and then and had to be helped – "by a very motherly lady" – to an antechamber to recover.

One of her excursions during this visit to London was to call on the county school she had taught in 1948. Miss Dorothy Fawn, the principal, and the children she had taught remembered her well; perhaps better than she had reckoned. They noticed that "Mrs Choy has no flower in her hair!" It was not because she had suddenly lost her love for flowers and their fragrance. To her, her dressing was not quite complete without the floral finishing touch. In her year as a teacher at the county school, she had befriended a florist near the school. She would stop to chat with the old woman, often buying a flower from her. On this day in 1953, she remembered the little flower-shop and thought she could again buy a flower from the florist. But alas, the shop was no longer there. So she had no flower for her hair that day. She certainly had not expected anyone other than herself to miss it.

To Mrs Choy, London had not lost its charm. Quite the contrary. London was even more captivating than on her last visit. When she first set foot in the city, it was in the immediate post-war year. London was almost in ruins; the ravages were painfully apparent. There was no escape from the omnipresent drabness. Shops were empty of wares. But she did notice that despite the lack of supplies, shopkeepers would bravely display the boxes – even when empty – rather prettily and neatly. And rationing was still on. The rationing in London had evoked painful memories of seeing the civilians of Singapore starving to death during the occupation years. (The Japanese occupation forces had enforced drastic rationing, but there just was not enough food to keep starvation at bay.)

When Mrs Choy arrived in London in 1946, what met her might well be the typical British stiff upper lip. She could not but notice and appreciate that despite understandable weariness and despondency in the immediate post-war, there were smiles and joviality. By the time she arrived for the Coronation, the London of 1953 was a fairyland. She was greeted by cleanliness, neatness, cheer and munificence. The city was magnificently decorated for the historic occasion. The euphoria was contagious. Everyone seemed so blissful; the shops so well-stocked. And Mrs Choy could not help but notice that all the women wore nylon stockings, a prized, rare commodity during the war years.

Mrs Choy, then a nominated Legislative Councillor, was in London as the sole representative of the Singapore Parliamentary Association. She appreciatively told one and all that it was the gallantry of her fellow councillors back home that had led to her presence in London for the historic celebration. Singapore's Legislative Council had twenty-five members of whom twenty-four were men. The twenty-four men had unanimously voted that Mrs Choy should represent them. So there she was. The official celebration started on 27 May 1953. The Commonwealth Parliamentary Associations throughout the British Commonwealth hosted a luncheon party for Princess Elizabeth, soon to be crowned Queen Elizabeth II, and her consort, Prince Philip, the Duke of Edinburgh. The venue was Westminster Hall with nearly eight hundred people in attendance.

Mrs Choy was right there in Westminster Abbey for the Coronation. Once again, she was like a schoolgirl, awe-struck and starry-eyed by the grandeur of it all. All that unfolded before her moved her deeply: the splendour of the building itself, the magnificence of the pageantry and not least of all, the service. The ethereal beauty of the church music, the unvoiced prayer of one and all were, to her, truly majestic and stirring.

In a radio interview upon her return to Singapore, she recalled vividly what she witnessed and her personal response to the Coronation: "Who could help but admire the grace, dignity and youthfulness of the Queen; the loveliness of the music; the charm of the Queen Mother; the brilliance of the coronets, the radiant loveliness of the princesses and the maids-of-honour, and the charming innocence of the page boys..."

1   Literally meaning riding gown; in South-east Asia, it is often referred to in the Cantonese dialect as cheongsam, meaning long gown.

2   During the Japanese occupation, both Sir Shenton (the Governor of the Straits Settlements and High Commissioner for the Malay States before the fall of Singapore and Malaya) and Lady Thomas were interned – separately. Sir Shenton was shipped out, first to Korea, then to Japan. His wife was interned in Singapore. At one stage, Mrs Choy was able to get some medicine and daily necessities to Lady Thomas. This act of kindness was not forgotten. After the war, as a token of her gratitude, Lady Thomas gave Mrs Choy an heirloom: a gold necklace of very fine Indian workmanship in the shape of a snake; for eyes, two rubies, while a third magnificent ruby dangled from the snake's open mouth. It had been given to Lady Thomas by her grandmother. Lady Thomas would not take no from Mrs Choy. Later, Mrs Choy in turn gave it to her eldest daughter as a twenty-first birthday present.

3   There were several hundreds of foreign women who were interned in Singapore for the duration of the occupation. In the wake of Double Tenth, a number of them were singled out by the *Kempeitai* for interrogation. Two of them were in the hands of the *Kempeitai* for five months. See *Destined Meeting* by Leslie Bell (Odhams Press, 1959) and *Dear Philip* by Freddy Bloom (Bodley Head, 1980).

4   Forty-three years later, on 11 October 1989, Mrs Choy would sit down to dinner on board the royal yacht *Britannia* as a guest of Queen Elizabeth II. The British monarch was in Singapore on a state visit.

5   The noted Russian-born London-based sculptress died in the early 1990s.

6   Back in Singapore, Mrs Choy was relieved to learn that Marie had joined the Teachers' Training College. Later, as a qualified teacher, Marie furthered her studies at the Froebel Educational Institute in London. Tragically, she was to die of cancer at thirty-one, leaving behind three very young children.

7   Now with the National Museum of Singapore.

IX

POLITICAL NAIVETE

A STOOL – a three-legged stool – was her emblem in the December 1950 Municipal election. And she lost.

When Mrs Choy returned to Singapore in December 1949 after her four-year stay in Britain, the change in Singapore was striking; apparent was not just the physical reconstruction of the war-ravaged island but also the attitude of its populace. The people's opinion of the British had changed irrevocably. They had been abandoned to fend for themselves during the Japanese occupation years. Now the people had a new lease of life; they were in a hurry to mend their disrupted lives and make their lot better. Singapore had been part of the Straits Settlements; the latter had ceased to exist, but Singapore was still a British colony. The peninsula had become the Federation of Malaya. But people in the streets tended to disregard political propriety; to many, Singapore and the peninsula to its north were seen as one entity. Indeed, many had relatives on both sides of the causeway that connected Singapore to its hinterland. The people of Malaya and Singapore were not prepared to complacently allow distant Westminster or Whitehall to rule them as before. Political consciousness seemed contagiously present.

On closer scrutiny, political aspirations could be divided along racial lines. Thus, very evident was Malay nationalism, especially across the causeway where the Malays had numerical superiority. The ethnic Chinese did not speak with one voice or see eye to eye. They were sharply divided among themselves – the English-educated versus the Chinese-educated. By and large, the English-educated did not wish for change. To the Chinese-educated, the former were the 'running dogs' of the British; 'bananas', yellow on the outside, white inside. Many of them could barely hold a conversation in any Chinese dialect or Mandarin. That alone was enough to alienate them from the majority of dialect-speaking Chinese.[1]

In the late 1940s, two political parties had come into being: the Progressive Party and the Labour Party. They were to dominate the political scene for just a while in the immediate post-war and pre-independence years. The Progressive Party was set up in August 1947 by lawyer C. C. Tan. He was considered an establishment figure and his party was seen as representative of mercantile interests. It was inaugurated just in time for it to contest in the first Legislative Council election held on 20 March 1948. Contesting against Independents, the Progressive won three out of the six contested seats. (To political analysts, the election was a farce. Of a potential electorate of 200,000, barely 11 per cent registered to vote.) The Labour Party was founded in 1948. Two future chief ministers were members of the Labour Party: David Marshall and after him, Lim Yew Hock.

At the end of 1950, Municipal Council elections were due. This council was a non-law-making body which was about to become the City Council when Singapore was raised to city status by royal charter in 1951. By the time Mrs Choy had returned to Singapore at the end of 1949, she was far more worldly-wise than before the war; but politics did not magnetise her. The Municipal election was, in fact, the first time she heard of the word 'election' as she was not in Singapore when the first poll to the Legislative Council took place. Unfortunately, she was not much good at saying no, especially when lawyer V. J. Mendes was persistent and persuasive. He convinced her that Singapore needed someone like her, an educated woman with keen interest in social services – she could not deny that – to sit on the council.

Mrs Choy stood as an Independent. Her constituency: Cairnhill or 'West Ward' as it was known. She did not know what she was in for. She had no platform, no advisers and little resources except for her willingness to do her best and her sincerity to convince the sceptical. She did not understand the profile of the constituency, one of relative wealth. She campaigned as best she knew, visiting house after house, but obviously failed to convince enough people in the ward that she should represent them. To her, it was a learning experience. Although poorer in the pocket, it was nevertheless rewarding in that she learnt a lot about people in the process. It was almost a relief to her, to leave the experience behind and concentrate on teaching the children of St Andrew's Junior School. But she was not off the hook yet.

The following year, 1951, she was rather taken aback when she was asked to accept nomination as an unofficial member of the Legislative Council. Her first reaction was to say no. She had lost one election and that was that. She did not want to be given a voice in another through the back door; least of all would she want to be there as a token female in the male-dominated assembly. (There was at that point one elected woman councillor.) But she was told that there was a definite vacuum in the assembly; she was needed to look after the interests of women and children. Since the area was of special concern to her, she gave in and accepted the nomination. It was not a job or a career; the council only sat once a month. The Governor's private secretary, Mike Gorrie, told her that the search for nominated councillors led to her because

Throughout your life, you have always put others before yourself and no words of mine can adequately describe the excellent service you have given to your country, your fellow men, and by no means least the thousands of St Andrew's pupils who had been moulded and inspired by your shining example.

Thus, Sir Franklin Gimson, the Governor, officially nominated Mrs Elizabeth Choy Su-Moi, the school teacher and social worker, to the assembly. The year after her nomination, before Sir Franklin relinquished his post as Governor, he wrote to her, stating:

I have always felt that my nomination of you as an unofficial member of the Legislative Council has been fully justified, and I wish to express my appreciation of the work which you are doing on behalf of the inhabitants of the colony.

In her second year, she became the only woman Legislative Councillor.[2] Mrs Choy was often called upon to speak and the one subject which she frequently addressed was political awareness – or ignorance – of the womenfolk in Singapore. Demographic data indicated that there were in fact more women than men on the island. Be that as it may, Mrs Choy highlighted that, of an estimated total of 300,000 eligible voters for the next election in 1955, 140,000 were female. But the electoral register had only 12,000 women. Much of the substance of the speeches she made during her one term in the council was echoed decades later by others. While fully concurring with Confucius on the crucial role of the family in society, while recognising the invaluable role played by women as home-makers in ensuring an ideal environment to nurture the next generation, she nevertheless urged women to take a greater interest in the goings-on outside of the home. They were also told that their contributions were needed in the professions and in politics. And they should exercise their right to choose by casting their votes during elections. Mrs Choy had learnt that the Tibetan word for woman actually means 'born inferior'. She noted that the attitude was prevalent in many parts of Asia. But that did not make it right. Not in the second half of the twentieth century; not when democracy had come to stay. It would be up to the women themselves to prove that they were anything but inferior. After all, were they not the 'better half?

Mrs Choy was also a role model to women in volunteer work.

In the 1950s, volunteers accounted for a sizeable force, especially so in internal security. Those were the days when ordinary law-abiding civilians – for example, civil servants and teachers – could well be singled out by terrorists to make a political statement in the bloodiest manner. Those were also the days when secret societies thrived, when political riots were common and labour strikes rowdy, if not violent. Mrs Choy became the belle of the battalion – otherwise known as 'Gunner Choy' – in the women's auxiliary of the Singapore Volunteer Corps, modelled on the British Women's Auxiliary Corps which had served with distinction during the Second World War. It was the then Governor, Sir Robert Black, who had suggested that with her involvement, more women would come forth. But as she ruefully recalls, the only ones she managed to recruit were nurses and teachers, mostly her friends and colleagues. The women were largely assigned to plot aircraft movements. It was not specially taxing but it had its moments. And she was promoted to the rank of second lieutenant for her contribution.

Mrs Choy treasured the experience gleaned during her years as an unofficial Legislative Council member. Not one to undertake anything in half measures, she did her utmost to justify her nomination. She spoke out on behalf of the poor, of the sufferings, frustrations and struggles of people for whom each day was a fight for survival. She urged for more social services; she pleaded for official support for family planning.[3] As an active social worker, there was excitement aplenty, but sadly, mostly from fires and floods. At one such natural disaster – when the devastating floods reached above one's waist and washed away countless squatters' huts – she noticed a young man's face, a face that stood out in the crowd, a face of youthful determination as he did his part lending a helping hand to the hapless flood victims. It was the face of Lee Kuan Yew.

On 21 November 1954, the People's Action Party, the PAP, came into being. In the 1955 Legislative Council election, twenty-five of the thirty-two seats were to be elected. Mrs Choy was glad that her term would soon be over; she would dearly love to devote more time to her family – by then, there were three very young daughters. But once again, she was approached to stand – this time, by the Progressive Party which had won six out of the nine elected seats in the 1951 election. The party wanted her to stand in Queenstown. Although she "flatly refused", she still allowed herself to be persuaded.

It was the infancy of democracy in Singapore. The franchise was still a new concept. With the prevailing high illiteracy rate, candidates were identified by symbols. These would be easily recognisable to even the simple-minded: a hat, an umbrella, a basket, a pair of spectacles, a house, a motor-car, a book, a box. When Mrs Choy first contested in the 1950 Municipal election, she drew a stool, a three-legged one. By the time she stood in the 1955 Legislative Council election, this practice had been dropped. Each candidate would be identified by the party's logo. The Progressive Party's logo was an orchid.

In a press interview reported in *The Sunday Times* of 7 November 1954, Mrs Choy was quoted as saying: "I thought I had done my bit in politics and that when the new Legislative Assembly is born, I would be able to retire. But the Progressive Party persuaded me to stand... by pointing out that they had no other woman candidate. That is the only reason I am contesting the election – because I feel the woman's point of view must be represented by someone." But once again, her naivete showed. The constituency was working class; the Progressive Party was identified with the rich.

In the months preceding the election, political temperature was feverish, dangerously so. The infamous and bloody Hock Lee bus riot of April-May 1955 was not the only headline-maker; there was another bus strike in February that year. Then there was the huge demonstration by students of Chinese-medium schools on the eve of the election.[4] There were other demonstrations and campaigns: Against the detention of trade unionists, against the Emergency Regulations and against the authorities' rumoured intention to replace the draconian Emergency Regulations which allowed detention without trial with another piece of legislation. (The agitators were suspicious of the authorities, that the latter might scrap the Emergency Regulations as a political move but repackage and retain the provision permitting detention without trial under another label.)[5]

It had been all in all an exhausting and costly experience for Mrs Choy. She had been upset by the untruths said about her by her political opponents, that she cared only for the wealthy. The mudslinging was very hurtful and bewildering to her. "In all my life, I had never quarrelled with anyone, never told a lie." She could not bring herself to retaliate. To speak ill of others to score points was asking too much of her. The campaign dragged on for several months. Candidates, even when representing specific political parties, were left very much to their own devices and had to fend for themselves. Mrs Choy had therefore to formulate her own policy and write it up, arrange for the printing of her own posters and pamphlets, get them distributed and then venture forth to canvas support. On the day of election, each candidate would have to provide transport for the voters from their homes to the voting centres. It could get quite disorderly. Inevitably, there would be the bullies around, arm-twisting voters into 'choosing' certain candidates – or else.

In the 1955 election, the PAP fielded four candidates and won three seats. Lee Kuan Yew, then thirty-two years of age, was elected to the seat for Tanjong Pagar. David Marshall's Labour Front – reconstructed from the Labour Party – took ten out of the seventeen seats it contested. One of them was Queenstown. Mrs Choy had lost. David Marshall was asked to form the government, a minority one in the thirty-two member Legislative Assembly, with him as the Chief Minister.

In the aftermath of the two elections she participated in, Mrs Choy could not but have reservations over the democratic process of vote-casting. Elections were meaningless until such time when the electorate became more politically sophisticated and more discerning. But she noted that, over the years, much had changed for the better. The chaotic political scenario of the 1950s belongs to history.

There were always those who would be wise after the fact. Thus, there were those who told her that she would have certainly won a seat if she had stood as an Independent. No matter. She was totally convinced that she was not meant for politics. But she also knew that she could contribute to society just as productively by moulding and nurturing the future citizens of the country as a teacher – a colossal responsibility, and one she cherished.

---

1   However, the ever pragmatic ethnic Chinese were mindful of the fact that to get good jobs, literacy in English made all the difference. Thus, increasingly, children form Chinese-speaking families were enrolled in schools that taught in English. By 1954, for the first time, enrolment in English-medium schools exceeded that of Chinese-medium schools.

2   The one and only elected woman Legislative Councillor, an Indian national, had vanished from Singapore. See Chapter XI.

3   In the fledgling days of the family planning movement, the stalwarts were all volunteers. A prime mover was Mrs Constance Goh Sai-Poh who launched the Family Planning Association (FPA) in 1949, using her husband's private medical clinic as its base. Despite opposition, chiefly from the Catholic Church, the volunteers were undaunted. Population growth was then averaging four percent; it dropped to 2.5 percent by 1964. This was still considered too high for Singapore. Constraints made it difficult for the FPA to expand its services without official support. In 1965, the FPA's clinical services were handed over to the government. By then, the Family Planning and Population Board had been established.

4   In 1957, the government acted to put an end to trouble-making rabble-rousing students and unionists. In one big swoop, several hundreds of Chinese-medium school students, trade union members, sympathisers, including a headmaster, were arrested one night. The late Lee Siow Mong, then Permanent Secretary for Education, noted in his autobiography *Words Cannot Equal Experience* (Pelanduk, 1985) that it "proved to be one of the most effective operations ever attempted..."

5   The Emergency Regulations came into force in 1948 when Singapore and Malaya came under a state of emergency.

X

THE PERFECT CHOICE

SHE TASTED HER FIRST DOUGHNUT in Canada, in Winnipeg, Manitoba Province. It was during her visit to the Red Cross Centre there. Her hosts were clearly delighted by her enjoyment of this popular western sugar-coated confection. A recipe to make thirty-five doughnuts was swiftly delivered to her with the reassurance that they could be easily prepared in any kitchen. For enhanced pleasure, noted a reminder at the end of the recipe, do not forget to 'dunk'.

Mrs Choy was first approached by the British Foreign Office when she was in London for the Coronation of Queen Elizabeth II. She, The Honourable Mrs Elizabeth Choy Su-Moi, Singapore's first and only woman nominated Legislative Councillor, was invited by the British Foreign Office to go on a three-month long lecture tour of North America, to explain the hopes and aspirations of Singapore and Malaya to the people of Canada and the United States of America. They wanted a convincing spokesperson, a goodwill ambassador and Mrs Choy was the perfect choice.

Mrs Choy was agreeable, but she had one condition. She would only do so if she were given first-hand exposure to life in Peninsular Malaya. Her knowledge of Singapore's hinterland, Malaya, was too sketchy. She needed an urgent update on the changes that had taken place during her four years away from the region. When she returned to Singapore at the end of 1949, the Emergency was on, covering both Singapore and the Federation of Malaya. She could not in all honesty extrapolate from her personal experience living in Singapore to cover the people living across the causeway.

The state of emergency had much to do with erstwhile heroes of the occupation years. The Malayan People's Anti-Japanese Army, whose members were remembered as the valiant and defiant fighters during those horrifying years, had their own vision of the ideal route to independence for Singapore and Malaya – the communist way. Labour, organised through unions, was the obvious vehicle through which to attack the establishment. Anti-British propaganda became increasingly provocative. When the British retaliated, the communists went underground in Singapore; across the causeway, on the peninsula, they opted for the jungle. On 16 June 1948, three European rubber estate managers were killed by guerillas in Sungei Siput, Perak. A state of emergency was proclaimed, covering the states of Perak and Johor. Two days later, it was extended to cover the whole of the peninsula. A week after, Singapore too came under the same proclamation. The Malayan Communist Party was outlawed. The Emergency Regulations and the harsh law that provided for detention without trial came into force. The state of emergency remained for twelve years.

Four years after the proclamation, guerillas in the jungle were still attacking the establishment and disrupting the livelihoods of ordinary folk with unabated intensity. In 1952, General Sir Gerald Templer was appointed High Commissioner of the Federation of Malaya; his predecessor, Sir Henry Gurney, had been assassinated.

To General Templer, it was plain that civilian communities scattered in remote pockets of the peninsula were natural prey to, and supporters (willingly or otherwise) of, the guerillas in the jungles. Severing the guerillas' access to such communities would be far more deadly effective than using all the military hardware at his command. And so the 'New Villages' – several hundreds of them, each one averaging about a thousand dwellers – came into ignominious existence. Whole hamlets were transplanted and surrounded by barbed wire; the residents' movements were restricted; strict curfews were enforced; identity cards were introduced; sentries were on duty twenty-four hours a day. In truth, these New Villages were probably not unlike internment camps.

Mrs Choy received the exposure she asked for. General Templer arranged for her to visit a number of 'black' pockets, areas identified as guerilla-infested; among them, the notorious Gua Musang in the State of Kelantan. An armoured train took her there. She saw life in the New Villages, witnessed the hardships borne by the villagers, but understood the need for such heavy-handed measures against seemingly harmless village folk. (Among the restrictions strictly enforced: rubber tappers were not allowed to bring any food with them when they left home for work each day before the crack of dawn – despite the fact that the tappers would not be returning home till they had completed their work many hours later. This was to prevent food from being supplied to the guerillas.) There were other programmes in Mrs Choy's itinerary, in the fields of welfare and children. She was introduced to Lady Templer's pet project, the Women's Institute, aimed at popularising handicraft as a cottage industry among the poorly educated housewives. At the end of a one-month tour of the peninsula, she felt adequately prepared to present Singapore and Malaya to the people of North America.

Mrs Choy had always enjoyed meeting people and making new friends. On the trip ahead, there was an added bonus – the opportunity to practise the French she first learnt in school. Her four years in Britain had removed whatever apprehension that there might otherwise have been for an Asian to address people of very different cultural backgrounds. Her British experience had opened her eyes to the ways of the West, to understand and appreciate the people and their culture. Of course, she was mentally prepared that North Americans might not be "just like" the Britons.

She left Singapore armed with facts and figures, not forgetting a map to pinpoint the region to her audience on the other rim of the vast Pacific Ocean. Singapore is such a micro-dot on a world map that it is not visible; the Malayan peninsula to its north is of respectable size, sufficient for its distinctive shape to be recognised. But few people in the West could identify the location of either Singapore or Malaya.

An array of appropriate gifts was prepared: Books, maps, handicraft-silverware and sarongs. Among the latter, a special gift for the First Lady of the United States of America, Mrs Dwight Eisenhower: a Kelantanese hand-woven sarong with a distinctive pattern known as *pucuk rebung*, patterned on the bamboo plants seen along the Kelantan River; sarongs with such patterns were worn only by Malay nobility. There was also a hand-woven sarong and a silver bracelet for Mrs Richard Nixon, wife of the Vice-President of the United States of America.

Then there was of course her own wardrobe of *qipao*, many made of batik with traditional motifs of the Malays. To complete her wardrobe and protect her from the bitter winter cold of North America, an exquisite coat made of Persian lamb's wool was loaned to her by Mrs Loke Yew of Cathay Organisation, a leading film distributor in the region. When she heard of Mrs Choy's trip, she had offered to lend her a suitable coat but Mrs Choy had declined. When Governor Sir John Nicoll learnt of this, he told Mrs Choy that she was not to leave Singapore without the coat. He recounted his personal experience of Canadian winter, when his trousers became iced. The coat made all the difference on the trip for, throughout her tour, the temperature in Canada was consistently well below freezing.

It was an exhausting but fulfilling and rewarding tour during the frigid months of early 1954. It was just as well that she already had years of practice as a teacher in delivering lectures. In between her speaking engagements would be many an interview. If her Washington DC diary was any indication of her schedule, the pace set for her was punishing – except that to her, it was exhilarating. Her schedule barely allowed a long weekend in the American capital. During that short span, she was on television and radio;

there were also press interviews to fit in. Then there was her official call on Mr Nixon. The Vice-President gave her a conducted tour of Capitol Hill. He escorted her into the Senate where a heated debate was on. It was Senator John Bricker who was vehemently opposing legislative amendments to restrict the President's treaty-making powers. Mrs Choy's brief appearance distracted his fellow senators and viewers in the public gallery, so too Senator Bricker as all eyes turned to take in the oriental vision at the side of the Vice-President.

While her schedule was carefully planned, it was not fail-proof. There was, for instance, the day when seven hundred women in Vancouver, British Columbia, were left waiting because Mrs Choy failed to keep her appointment. She was the innocent victim of a delayed flight from Calgary, Alberta. On her final leg home, someone neglected to book her flight to Singapore from San Francisco, but that meant that she had two engagement-free days in that picturesque Californian city. Apart from these occasions, she was able to keep to her extremely tight schedule, to the amazement of not a few.

For her talks – often on 'Singapore, the Great International Meeting Place of Peoples and Cultures' or 'Educating Asia's New Generation' – she would start with a bit of geography, pointing out the exact location of Singapore and Malaya on the world map and giving the relative distances to various countries her foreign listeners were more familiar with. Then, some history. On what existed before the arrival of the British, the Dutch and the Portuguese; and the 1819 founding of modern Singapore by Sir Thomas Stamford Raffles. She would also touch on the political evolution of Singapore and Malaya. The threat of communism could not be ignored. Mrs Choy explained to her audience the events that led to the promulgation of the Emergency and the proscription of the Malayan Communist Party. She emphasised that the communists who operated from the jungle of Malaya were not leading a nationalist patriotic movement by undermining British presence through the disruption of the economies of Singapore and Malaya.

In urbanised Singapore, she would add, there were, undeniably, sympathisers. Official estimates put the figure at around two thousand. While the movement had gone underground, its dark presence was very much felt by the people of Singapore. Assassins boldly murdered a Chinese businessman in his office, taking time to leave behind propaganda leaflets glorifying the movement. A grenade was thrown at a former governor of Singapore. Fortunately, it had a defective shell. An estimated $13 million went up in smoke when arson was committed against a factory in Singapore. Among the sympathisers were school children, largely those of the Chinese-medium school. By then, 15 per cent of Singapore's annual budget was going to security. Across the causeway, in the Federation of Malaya, the Emergency was costing $1 million a day.

Military services, full-time as well as on a volunteer basis, had been set up in Singapore. There were three: The Royal Malayan Navy, the Malayan-Australian Air Force and the Singapore Volunteer Corps. Mrs Choy herself was a member of the last, in the Women's Air-plotting Group. There was also the Royal Naval Volunteer Reserve, a part of the British Navy. It was the beginning of Singapore's national service enlistment. She fully concurred with the opinion of a budding political leader in Singapore, that "no country is ready for self-government till it is able to put itself, from its own resources, in a position of self-defence". In a nutshell, Singapore, a vibrant Asian city, had thrived on its geographic location and nature's gift of an excellent harbour. There was much the city-state could be justly proud of, but there was much more to be done, to ensure its rightful place in the sun. She was confident that the youthful population, under the able leadership of a fast emerging local political leadership, would attain peace, prosperity and independence via the democratic route.

Mrs Choy's schedule literally had her talking her way from the east coast to the west coast of North America. Although Canada, like Singapore and Malaya, was (and is) a member of the British Commonwealth, many of the Canadians she addressed were, till then, only vaguely aware of where she came from; they were even more vacuous about the political aspirations of Asians in the post-war era. For some, she was possibly the first oriental person they met face to face. She adapted and re-focused her topics according to the specific audience.

Many of her speaking engagements involved women's organisations: The Women's Canadian Club of London, Ontario; the Victoria Business and Professional Women's Club; University Women's Club of Vancouver; the Ottawa Women's Canadian Club; the Chinese Women's Club of Los Angeles and many more. Mrs Choy made sure that she would have her audience interested, not just by talking about the people's political aspirations and the socio-economic development of her part of the world, not just by describing the multi-racial population back home. She enlivened her talks with her one-woman show. Clothes and fashions, she knew, were of universal fascination; she modelled the costumes of Asia herself. Not only did she bring her special *qipao* – the one which she wore for the Coronation – she had with her sarongs and saris. She would transform herself by, in turn, deftly wrapping a two-metre sarong around her waist and draping a five-and-half-metre sari on her body.

In addition to women's groups, she also spoke to undergraduates. Among the colleges she visited were the University of Washington and the Seattle University. She also addressed the University of Manitoba and the University of Saskatchewan where a faculty member, Mr A. Anstensen, in a note of appreciation, stated:

> *Your talk to our students was very much appreciated. It is very refreshing, in these days of hectic and wild-eyed propaganda by table-thumping apostles of various shades of pink and red, to get such a calm and rational assurance that intelligent and sane Asians are themselves busily at work, building the only solid foundation on which democracy can be established in their countries.*

In Toronto, Canada, the Trinity College was keen to have her speak to students of its women's college, St Hilda's. It so happened that the principal of the college, an English woman, Katherine M. Darroch, had spent some time in Singapore and was particularly keen to meet Mrs Choy. Following the all-girl meeting, the provost arranged for another gathering of "a carefully chosen group of our most able students" – both men and women – to meet her. For the meetings, Mrs Choy was asked to address her very serious audience, keenly interested in the political awakening of developing countries, on the matter of Singapore's and Malaya's progress towards self-govemment. She was well armed with fact-sheets on the subject.

Soldiers: the army and air force commands of Western Canada were on her schedule too. Feedback on her talks, sent by the Canadian Department of National Defence to her sponsors, the British Information Services, was that the lectures were "the most successful in a long time." The local media noted that she was one of the very few women ever invited to breach male bastions like the Canadian Club of Toronto. (Perhaps in the eyes of men, male chauvinists in particular, the fact that she was heralded as a 'war heroine' had raised her gender status to at least equal to any man.)

There were some familiar faces on the tour. Among them, Mrs Malcolm MacDonald, wife of the Commissioner-General of Southeast Asia. In anticipation of her husband's retirement, Canadian-born Mrs MacDonald had brought her children to Ottawa, the Canadian capital, to await his arrival. At the time of Mrs Choy's tour, Mrs MacDonald had already waited for almost two years. Mr and Mrs Nixon she had met during their Asian tour in 1953. ("They were such nice people, so courteous," recalled Mrs Choy. In the decades ahead, there would be the occasional exchange of correspondence with the Nixons.) The Governor of New York, Mr Thomas E. Dewey, was yet another familiar face. He too had visited Singapore earlier, in 1951. Mrs Choy brought back a recipe for date loaf, courtesy of Mr Dewey's mother.

Perhaps the happiest encounter was the surprise meeting with someone she had not expected to ever see again. While in British Columbia, she received a message informing her that a Mr Dunlop would like to call on her. The only Mr Dunlop she could recall was her prison cell-mate whom she assumed had died at the hands of their jailors. But it was indeed the very same person, very much alive and as hairless as before. He was the one who predicted that Mrs Choy would not only survive the war but would become famous and people would read about her in the newspapers. And there she was, now The Honourable Mrs Elizabeth Choy Su-Moi, making headlines in newspapers, being heard over radio and seen on television on the other side of the globe. He had in fact read about her lecture tour of North America and had travelled hundreds of kilometres just to see her again and to tell her to her face: "I told you so." To Mrs Choy, it was such delightful serendipity.

During her American sojourn, the organisers of her tour inter-mingled home stays with hotels. In Seattle, Washington State, for instance, Senator and Mrs Clinton S. Harley were her hosts. Such stays made a lot of difference to the itinerant ambassador of goodwill from Singapore. It not only gave her further insights into the way of life of North Americans but inevitably, her effervescent personality left a deeper impression on the people she met at close quarters.

There were invitations to host her from total strangers who had learnt of her lecture tour from the media. A Mr A. B. Carey of Los Angeles wrote to invite her to stay with him and his wife, should the Californian city be on her itinerary. It appeared that they had lived in Malaya for many years, from 1909 to 1931. In his letter, he told Mrs Choy that he and his brother had opened a "big estate" near Port Swettenham named Carey Island. There were others who wrote to her asking for little favours. A hand-written note from a Mrs E. Beanard of Brooklyn, New York, asked ever so politely if Mrs Choy would be "so kind as to aid me in my stamp collection."

At the end of her lecture tour, she could, on a personal level, count many new friends on the North American continent. She certainly brought back many personal souvenirs as people had spontaneously pressed into her hands badges and brooches they had been wearing, wanting her to take these home. These became her much-treasured American collection.

There was no dearth of response to Mrs Choy's official solicitation on behalf of the Women's Institute of Malaya. Offers to send materials needed by the institute came from organisations as well as individuals. Cartons of cloth, threads and needles soon headed for the institute's headquarters in Kuala Lumpur. The first shipments arrived just when Sir Gerald and Lady Templer were leaving the country. The latter penned a note of thanks in appreciation of Mrs Choy's fruitful North American tour. Separately, boxes of second-hand toys arrived; these were in response to Mrs Choy's lament that to many children of Singapore and Malaya, toys were a luxury they could not enjoy in their young lives.

There was considerable curiosity about Mrs Choy in the West. Advance publicity about her would of course introduce her as a war heroine, a lawmaker, an educator and a social worker. Often, there would be a house full of eager listeners. She captivated her audience with her eloquent delivery of dry facts and figures; she enraptured them with her one-woman show. And people wondered aloud about her fluent English. (But alas, despite all the press releases on the woman from the Orient, there were still those who could not get her name right. In one newspaper, she was 'Mrs Moy'; in another, 'Mrs Su'; in yet another, she was 'Madam Elizabeth Moy Choy'.) The French newspapers also gave her coverage, although she did not get much of a chance to practise her French.

The press fell under the spell of this oriental woman. Media coverage was generous and complimentary; in some cases, downright flattering. But when it came to describing the *qipao*, the western journalists lost their flair for words. One typical clumsy attempt went like this: "... tight, form-fitting, high-collar Chinese style, with side-split skirt ... " A rather amusing attempt to describe the garment came from one of Mrs Choy's American hostesses, the wife of the Governor of New York State. In a note she wrote to Mrs Choy, Mrs Anne Dewey quoted herself as describing Mrs Choy's dress as "tube-like" to a curious friend who missed meeting Mrs Choy but wanted details of the guest-speaker, especially on what she wore. Mrs Dewey went on to note: "How she got into it I could not see, but it looked as though she pulled it right over her head to just the right length with a slit in (*sic*) bottom that allowed you to walk gracefully...."

However, journalists had no trouble finding the words and adjectives to compliment Mrs Choy. Here are samples from press clippings: "a beautiful heroine", "serene face of the delicate, slender and beautiful Chinese Malayan", "pretty ambassador of goodwill", "charming law-maker, social worker and war heroine", "a serene and charming war heroine, politician and world traveller."

The western perception of the oriental form was, well, rather astonishing. The broad-shouldered Mrs Choy was all of 1.68-metres tall in her bare feet. (Shoes came with rather high heels – seven to eight centimetres in the 1950s.) She was statuesque for a Chinese woman; not at all short compared to Caucasian women. The fact that she stood shoulder to shoulder with many of the western women she met on the tour had obviously escaped notice. What the press saw was quite something else: "petite", "diminutive, as dainty as a Dresden shepherdess... ", "tiny heroine", "small and dainty", "a dainty heroine", "a diminutive lady member of the Legislative Assembly."

Compliments should go to the Canadian journalist of *The Telegram*, Toronto, who was the odd one out in getting closer to reality, describing Mrs Choy as: "tall and slim... did not look like a rugged hero of tyranny and torture...."

Doubtless, Mrs Choy's personality had much to do with the warm and positive response accorded her wherever she went. In New York, a weekly chose her as Woman of the Week after her talks in that city. Her personality was noted by a male bastion, the Royal Canadian Air Force (RCAF). In a letter of thanks addressed to Mrs Choy, Dr Leslie A. Glinz, Current Affairs Adviser, Department of National Defence of Canada, informed her that the Winnipeg-based RCAF found her lecture on Singapore most interesting. He was also pleased to add: "Perhaps you would like to hear, also, that they were captivated by the personality of the speaker." And in Dr Glinz's opinion: "The government of Singapore was well served by its ambassador."

Opportunities for Mrs Choy to do her bit in correcting distorted images of Singapore in the minds of some people on the other rim of the Pacific Ocean did not only take place in a formal setting. There were opportunities presented during chance meetings along the kerb, for instance. There was the question asked of her by a stranger: "Are you from Singapore?" When Mrs Choy answered in the affirmative, the response from the North American was: "Well, Singapore isn't that bad then. The impression we got was that because Singapore is on the trade route, it must be a city of sin."

At the end of her three-month talkathon, the verdict, based on feedback sent to the British Foreign Office and as conveyed to Mrs Choy, was, "A roaring success."

In an interview in Singapore published in the *New Nation* of 12 February 1971, Mrs Choy summarised her own impressions of the people of the West:

"The Americans are always on the move. They seldom seem to be content and are constantly searching for happiness. The Canadians are more sedate and steadier. They appear to be a more settled people. The English are a reserved lot but they are very sure of themselves. I find they make the best friends."

XI

A LIVING SAINT

"A LIVING SAINT" – to people who know and admire her, Elizabeth Choy Su-Moi is this and more. The first person to describe her so was someone who knew her intimately, having lived under the same roof as Mrs Choy for thirty-three years. This was her sister-in-law, Madam Choy Yuet Kum, her husband's eldest sister. Madam Choy had married at the age of nineteen into a Sarawakian family and lived in Sibu after marriage. After the demise of her husband just two years later, her in-laws suggested that she move to China where the family had property and where she could live free from want. This she did. Then came the victory of the Chinese Communist Party in 1949 and the birth of the People's Republic of China. When the Kuomintang of the Republic of China led by Generalissimo Chiang Kai-Shek fled to the island of Taiwan, the widow too fled: to the island of Singapore. She was childless, homeless and practically penniless.

When Mrs Choy heard of her plight, she saw as an obvious solution that her widowed sister-in-law should live at Mackenzie Road. Not only did she provide her with a home, she handed the whole household to her, appointing her mistress of her home. Mrs Choy made it clear to one and all that her sister-in-law was in charge of the running of the household and the supervision of the two live-in maids. And so for all of thirty-three years they lived harmoniously under the same roof. Mrs Choy admits that there were occasions when she did not quite agree with her sister-in-law – perhaps over the upbringing of her three little daughters or the performance of the maids – but she allowed the momentary annoyance to pass without voicing it. Before the sister-in-law died in 1983 at the age of eighty-four, she told everyone that Mrs Choy was truly a living saint.

Mr and Mrs Choy Khun Heng adored their three daughters, all adopted in the 1950s. First came Bridget, Wai Fong (Wisdom and Fragrance), born in 1950, the Year of the Tiger. Her natural parents were very distressed even before the birth, for they knew the baby would be born in the Tiger Year. They were firm believers of the lunar zodiac and its repercussions on fate and fortune. If the baby were a girl, it would be disastrous for the family. (If it were a boy, it would be quite all right.) But there was a way out; all would be well if the baby girl were given up for adoption. Mrs Choy was asked and she happily accepted the offer of becoming an instant mother. Within twenty four hours of her birth, Mrs Choy became Bridget's mother.

Two years later came Wai Ling (Wisdom and Melody), Lynette. Her natural parents, both in domestic service to town planner Denis Komlosey, felt that they could not afford to raise the latest addition to their family, their eighth. Their predicament was aggravated by the mother's frail health. It was the Komloseys who consulted Archdeacon Robin Woods; the latter in turn approached Mrs Choy.

At that time, Mrs Choy was in financial difficulty, having just been cheated by an unscrupulous woman. Much as she loved children, she was understandably reluctant to take on the responsibility of bringing up another child. But the Archdeacon impressed upon her that he wanted to ensure the baby was adopted by the right family – not just any family – and he felt the Choys would be just right. Mrs Choy compromised. She suggested that the Archdeacon and the natural parents should try to look for suitable alternative foster parents for the baby; if they failed to do so after a fortnight, she would be happy to have the child. And so Lynette joined the Choy family and became Bridget's little sister.

The third of the Choys' children is really a niece, the eighth or ninth child of Mr Choy's youngest sister. The natural parents were in financial straits and planned to give away the latest addition when born. They asked Mrs Choy if she would care to adopt the baby, if it were a boy. The natural parents assumed that since the Choys already had two girls, they would surely not want another girl. But to their surprise, Mrs Choy and her husband made it clear that they would love to have the baby, boy or girl. And so Wai Fun (Wisdom and Beauty), Irene, became the youngest in the family.

The Choys took great delight in the girls; they adored each and every one of them as they arrived at two-yearly intervals. Mrs Choy, then the only nominated woman Legislative Councillor, would not have hesitated giving up her seat, if only some other woman would come forward to speak on behalf of women and children. Already in her forties, she wanted so much to indulge herself as a mother. In an interview reported in *The Sunday Times*, 7 November 1954, she said: "My three children have brought me untold joy and pleasure – I can never have enough of domesticity; I find it so soothing." The councillor and full-time school teacher made it public that she was one woman who actually enjoyed housework, be it scrubbing, cleaning, cooking, sewing or decorating and rearranging the furniture. But there was no one to relieve her of her non-domestic extra-teaching responsibilities.

Despite her heavy commitments outside of the home, she was a committed parent. To her, her most important responsibility was to give each child as good an education as there was. She was determined that each of her girls would be given the opportunity to develop her full potential. She imparted to them the values she believed in. (And the maxims she lived by; an oft-repeated one: "Unless you can think of something good to say about a person, it is better not to say anything at all.") When the girls were growing up, she often told them that she would have no material wealth to bequeath them, but she hoped that their upbringing would have inculcated the right values and strength of character for them to face the challenges of life.

The year Mrs Choy was cheated of $10,000 – a large amount to her – it was a double tragedy. It was the early 1950s and she was barely acquainted with the con-woman, an Indian lawyer who had stood for the Legislative Council election of 1951 and had in fact won a seat. (Mrs Choy, who did not take part in this election, was later nominated to the Council by the Governor.) Perhaps the woman had sized Mrs Choy up as a "born sucker" who would fall for any sob-story. Thus, this woman, known to Mrs Choy as Mrs Menon, spun a convoluted tale to convince Mrs Choy of her pressing need for a guarantor, to enable her to get a desperately needed loan of $10,000. She swore by all that she held sacred that she would settle the loan in a very short time. She was not asking Mrs Choy for money; all she needed of Mrs Choy was her signature on the guarantee form. Mrs Menon seemed so reassuringly frank; she even confidently – and convincingly – gave Mrs Choy an exact date when she would no longer be in need of the loan facility.

Mrs Choy, ever ready to help anyone in need, did not for a moment doubt the woman's integrity. She agreed to stand as Mrs Menon's guarantor. That of course gave the woman the time she needed to skip town – to home in India – before the loan was due for repayment. Later, a story was related to Mrs Choy that when Mrs Menon arrived in India and opened her luggage for customs inspection, they were found to be filled with currency notes. Whether there was any veracity in that story, Mrs Choy was far too distraught to care. The finance company had turned to her as the guarantor when the borrower failed to settle the loan once it became due. But Mrs Choy did not have the money to meet the amount. Fortunately, there were decent and caring people around. Upon hearing of her plight, a friend wrote out a cheque and got the finance company off her back.

But the matter of course did not end there. Mrs Choy could not reward her friend by absconding too. Her only valuable worldly possession then was her home in Mackenzie Road. When the war ended, it was barely a shell. The owner refused to spend money on badly needed repairs on the bombed and looted two-storey terrace house. To the Arab Street merchant, the paltry rent he collected did not justify expenditure on repairs. He offered to sell it and the Choys bought it for $10,000. (And spent at least twice that amount on repairs.) She mortgaged the house to repay her kind-hearted friend who had paid the guarantee sum.

Being cheated at this point of time was doubly painful to Mrs Choy as she had just been offered a Teacher Training Grant by the United States of America to study the country's educational system and facilities for six months. The offer was a golden opportunity to one ever keen to learn; she had in fact accepted it and was looking eagerly forward to leaving in early 1953. However, under the circumstances, she felt compelled to withdraw her acceptance. Going on the tour meant taking leave without pay, and with the mortgage on her shoulders, she could not afford to be without her monthly salary for six months. To her, there was no choice. She had to turn the grant down.

Despite this awful experience, Mrs Choy never lost faith in people. She would quote a saying she found in a diary and take solace in it: "It is better to trust and be cheated than to distrust." She also found reassurance in the generosity of people who rallied round her. There was no shortage of offers to clear the mortgage on her behalf. Ambassador Elmer Newton of the United States of America offered to contact his personal friends to pay off the loan. "I would like you to meet the American people and also for the American people to meet you," he had urged. But Mrs Choy was adamant: "No, I have been foolish; I must bear the consequences, sad as it may be." There were about a dozen other offers from people in Singapore but she turned each and everyone down. It was her folly; she felt that only she should pay for it. It took her fourteen years to do so.

Doubtless there were those who told her that she should have known better. Among them, her father. (Her husband only learnt of what had happened after the house was mortgaged. It was one of the very rare occasions when the normally good-natured man was livid.) But she did not know better. Again and again she would fall prey to society's leeches. The matter of the $10,000 guarantee certainly did not stop her from extending a helping hand to others who convinced her that they were in dire need of help. She would remain gullible, easily convinced and moved by sad stories. The fame of her generosity went beyond the shores of Singapore.

A couple of years after Mrs Menon left Mrs Choy $10,000 poorer, there came a fabulous two-page hand-written letter from East Khandesh, India, penned by one G. M. Bhavalkar. After a two-paragraph preamble in which the writer informed Mrs Choy that he was a sixty-three-year-old man with four "minor girls" and that no member of his family was working, he went on to write:

> Learnt from reliable source that Mrs Elizabeth Choy of
> Singapore is very kind hearted, generous minded and always
> read (sic) to help poor family who is in distress no sooner the
> grievances put to your feet and hence approached to your feet
> such a long distant for Monetary help and oblige (sic).

The writer concluded with instructions on how he would like Mrs Choy to live up to her reputation. She could send an Imperial Bank of India cheque to the branch closest to where he was, or she could send him a postal order, uncrossed, in sterling pounds. Mrs Choy sent him $10 or $20.

Often, it was more than a helping hand or some money; she would cheerfully offer her roof too, not just to relatives, but to almost anyone. She would take in destitutes and would be let down again and again by the very people she helped unquestioningly. There was, for example, an Indian boy who begged Mrs Choy to take him in. He was 'Paul' to everyone in the Choy family. Second daughter Lynette recalled that he and his family lived just across the street from the Choys, in a two-storey detached house that had degenerated into a slum in which many families lived in squalor.

He had told Mrs Choy that his parents refused to send him to school, but he very much wanted to go, to be educated and be somebody.

So Paul moved in and lived with the Choys, partook of their meals, all free of charge, until he was through with learning and ready for employment. Mrs Choy went one step further and secured a job in the civil service for him; then she pointed out that it was time for him to go back to his parents. Civil servants were required to declare their debts, if any. It turned out that somewhere in his murky past, Paul owed others money – gambling debts – or so he told Mrs Choy. He needed a loan from Mrs Choy to clear his arrears, so that he could take up the job she had secured for him. Although she did not have the money to spare, typically, she made his problem her problem and borrowed the sum he asked for so that he could start life afresh with a clean slate. That was the last Mrs Choy saw of him.

Towards the end of the 1950s, the Choys again found themselves providing free board and lodging – this time, to a Eurasian woman. Initially, she was an occasional visitor; but before long, she became a 'house-guest'. The woman, whom the children addressed as 'Mrs Jansen', was probably in her thirties. Bridget and Lynette remember her as a rather "fun and plump woman" who would make them laugh with her clowning. At one stage when she had a flat in the Orchard Road area, she would, on occasion, take the girls there. Perhaps she never revealed her profession to the senior Choys but Lynette had seen her massaging visitors; sometimes, the young girls would be 'shooed' out of the room when the massage session was on.

Mrs Jansen and her missing husband must have been quite a pair. It seemed that when they were courting, each had given the other the impression that he/she was wealth-laden. Thus they found each other irresistible. But after the romancing and the exchange of vows "for better or for worse... till death do us part", they discovered, to their mutual horror, that it was definitely going to be for the worse. Each had expected to wallow in a blissfully hedonistic life of luxury sponging off the other. When the truth was out, neither party was about to wait for death to end their togetherness. The husband took off; the wife sought shelter with Mrs Choy. Again, Mrs Choy could not say no. And so this woman moved in to live off the Choys indefinitely. But that was not all.

Mrs Jansen openly admired an amethyst ring worn by Mrs Choy. She asked to borrow it for a social engagement as it would, according to Mrs Jansen, complement and complete her dressing for the occasion. Typically, Mrs Choy readily consented and parted with her ring. She never got it back. It would, of course, never occur to her to ask for its return. (Mrs Choy 's sister-in-law was far more cautious. When asked to lend her diamond ring, Madam Choy gave a flat no.)

The hospitable Mrs Choy allowed Mrs Jansen access to every part of the house and the house-guest obviously made herself very much at home. Not only did she have access to all the rooms, she assumed she was welcome to look into the cupboards too. Not just look, but to help herself to anything in them. Even the supremely tolerant and forgiving Mrs Choy was upset when Mrs Jansen decided to augment her own wardrobe and supply of undergarments by recycling her benefactress' clothes. Thus, she helped herself to some of Mrs Choy's *qipao*, and made panties out of them! Among those she cut up were the two silk *qipao* from Mrs Choy's wedding trousseau, the very ones she had worn in 1946 to Buckingham Palace.

Mrs Choy was not one for locks and keys but there was one locked item, an old trunk dating back to her St Monica's years in the 1920s. To someone on the prowl for anything valuable to pilfer, this must be it. It was locked; therefore, whatever therein must be valuable. It was quite some time after Mrs Jansen had finally left the Choy household when the loss was discovered. Whether it was Mrs Jansen who stole it, the thief was in for disappointment. The trunk contained mostly old family photographs, personal letters and documents, including Mrs Choy's family tree, and some clothes.[1] They were of immense sentimental value to Mrs Choy; pretty worthless to anyone else.

Among the things pilfered from the Choy household was an

oil painting by an English artist which Mrs Choy had posed for in 1949, a full figure nude highlighting her back. She had liked it very much and the artist was kind enough to let her have it. It had yet to be framed when it disappeared from Mackenzie Road. Gone too was the sword left behind in 1942 by the Japanese soldier who had attempted rape.

Mercifully, there was enough honesty around to make up for the misdeeds of the deceitful and ungrateful. Mrs Choy remembered well a trishaw-rider who, in the wake of a terrible fire in Geylang in 1953, was among those rendered homeless. Mrs Choy responded to a public appeal to provide temporary shelter to the victims. She took in the trishaw-rider and his family of five or more children. In due course, when alternative housing was made available, this man and his family left. Later, Mrs Choy heard that because of illness, he could no longer pedal a trishaw and had become a fortuneteller instead. One day, she chanced upon him in the street, plying his new profession, complete with a pair of caged Java sparrows to unravel the designs of heaven for the mortals on earth, in exchange for fifty cents per reading. She was of course not quite serious when she asked him to read her fortune. After all, as a practising Christian, she should not believe in divining. But the man surprised her by telling her that as she had been kind to him before, he had to be honest with her. The truth was, he said, he really could not divine anything; it was all a bluff. Instead of censuring him for making a living by telling lies, preying on others' superstition, Mrs Choy was so impressed by his outburst of honesty that she gave him five dollars.

She is unlikely to forget the three ethnic Indian friends – one a doctor, the others school teachers – who would, during the nightmarish years of the Japanese occupation, visit her family every few days to check if they had enough food. There was also the doctor Mrs Choy had befriended when she and her husband were running the hospital canteen before their arrest. This doctor remained a life-long friend, happy to take care of Mrs Choy's children's medical needs, but would never accept payment for his professional service.

In the days when she was learning the Malay language, she made it a point of reading *Berita Harian*, the news daily in Malay, to improve her command of the national language. But she did not have to buy the newspaper because a doctor and his lawyer wife would give their copy to her. It did not amount to much in dollars and cents, especially to two professionals and a used copy at that, but to Mrs Choy, the thoughtful gesture was deeply appreciated.

Mrs Choy has always had a penchant for pithy quotations. She has a store of these, many, not surprisingly, from the Bible. But not all. Among her favourites, are: from Confucius, "Do not do unto others what you do not wish them do to you," and from Jesus, "Do unto others what you would others do unto you."

---

1   When Mrs Choy recounted this incident in Volume IV Number One of *Intisari* in the mid-1960s, she thought her wedding gown was in the misappropriated trunk. Later, she she was relieved to find that it had been spared. Since then, this gown has been repurposed by her as a christening gown for a grandchild.

XII

GOD CAN WAIT

"GOD CAN WAIT, Poh Lin can't." To Mrs Choy, it was as simple as that. As a statement, it did not allow room for 'buts'. There were probably quite a number of people who had, at one time or other, been the recipient of this reply from Mrs Choy. For this was her standard response to those – concerned family-members and well-meaning friends – who tried to persuade her to break her appointments with Poh Lin. They perhaps wished to invite Mrs Choy for an outing which they believed she would enjoy. Mrs Choy had always enjoyed outings. Age did not diminish her sense of adventure or her interest in life. As a widow, a grandmother and an octogenarian, she was as active as she was decades before. But she was always very precise about her priorities; that never changed. If she had made an appointment with Poh Lin, then she had to keep it. She did not make an exception, even if the invitation involved the church. God, the deeply pious Mrs Choy contended, would understand. God, she said repeatedly, can wait. Poh Lin couldn't. And Poh Lin did not understand.

Maria Theresa Chan Poh Lin, born in Singapore in 1945, was blind, deaf and almost mute. She came to the world with normal faculties. Illness – possibly meningitis – disabled her irreversibly. By the time she turned fourteen, her world had become permanently dark and silent. With her hearing gone, her speech rapidly deteriorated. An only child, Poh Lin lived with her parents in abject poverty, in the midst of the infamous death-houses in the notoriously unsalubrious Sago Lane of Chinatown. The poor who were near death were sent to these commercially-run places to die.

The area was cluttered with rows of old and dilapidated shop-houses of two to three storeys, a relic of the British administration's decades of indifference to the housing needs of the low-income masses. The Chans' living quarters were a cubicle, up an unlit, rickety wooden staircase. No natural light could filter in. Thus, day or night, it was almost pitch-dark, as with the other cubicles in the row. Even the sighted had to grope their way about. In the Chans' cubicle was a wooden bed which took up practically all the space there was. Their meagre worldly belongings were stacked in one corner of the bed. Poh Lin slept beneath.

To Poh Lin's parents, there was nothing to be done for her. It was just their bad luck to not only have no son, but to have their one and only daughter become inflicted with such terrible multiple handicaps. Poh Lin's father was an indifferent parent and an unreliable provider for the family. Work did not interest him. Poh Lin's mother, a longsuffering and uncomplaining woman, worked as a dish-washer at a nearby restaurant. She struggled on and did her best by Poh Lin. How the child felt about her situation no one knew. She just kept crouched in one corner of the family's cubicle, out of people's way and ate whatever food her mother fed her. Then Mrs Choy came into her life.

It was the mid-1950s. Slowly but surely, more and more social services were coming on stream in Singapore. By 1956, Singapore was ready to invest in a school specially for the visually handicapped, to educate and train them not only to be self-reliant and literate, but also to contribute productively to the community and country. It was pioneering work. The search for a principal led to Mrs Choy, the perennial social worker. No matter how busy she was, she and social work had been inseparable. Permission was sought from St

Andrew's, the school where she taught, to release her to serve as the founding principal of the Singapore School for the Blind. She was to remain as the school's principal until 1960.

There was much to learn, but there was no expertise in Singapore. The closest sources of practical knowledge were in the Federation of Malaya. Just across the causeway, there was in Johor Baru the Princess Elizabeth School; then there was the Gurney Training Centre in Kuala Lumpur. The most experienced institution was in Penang, the St Nicholas School for the Blind which had pioneered care of the blind in the region. Singapore's school started with two expatriate teachers while Singaporeans were recruited and sent to Britain for specialised training.

If anyone had assumed that parents of disabled children would be pleased and relieved that special facilities were available in Singapore to educate their blind children, to train them to be as independent as possible – they would have been quite wrong. Some parents were ashamed of the fact that they had blind children; they would rather keep them out of the public eye. There were also the protective parents who likewise wished to keep their children at home to prevent them from getting ridiculed and hurt by the callous of the world. Mrs Choy soon realised that families and guardians of blind children were the greatest obstacle to the school's enrollment drive. Information pamphlets and publicity through the media did not seem to work. Visits by public figures and newsmakers – such as that of Prince Philip, the Duke of Edinburgh, in 1957 – did little to reshape parental attitude.

Undaunted, the indefatigable Mrs Choy had to personally canvass (almost like her political stumping days) for the school by seeking out families with blind children, to convince them that they should send their children to the school as boarders. She explained that the children would be taught to read and write, and there would also be handicraft classes. She was met with scepticism, the usual response being "what's the point ..." or "what's the use ..." and that she was quite mad to tell them that the blind could "read and see" with their finger-tips. There were parents who, accustomed to caring for their handicapped children, assumed that they were the only ones capable of doing so. Such was the case with the Malay couple with a blind son who visited the school to see for themselves the facilities available and to talk to Mrs Choy. The father was ready to give his consent to have his son stay at the school; but the dire prospect of leaving her poor, blind boy behind as a boarder was too much for the mother. "She cried and howled hysterically until she fainted there and then."

Often, Mrs Choy depended on information from people who would tell her that there was a blind child at such and such an address. Off she would go to recruit the child for her school. One day, she was told of a deaf and blind girl in Sago Lane. And so, among the houses of death, Elizabeth Choy found Chan Poh Lin.

Poh Lin's parents held the negative attitude of many parents of disabled children and were resigned to their fate in having such a child. But they were probably relieved that somebody actually wanted to care for their daughter. The father claimed that Poh Lin had been attending school until she fell ill, but he could not even give the name of the school, certainly not one that existed. When pressed for information, he merely waved his arm vaguely. Mrs Choy's exhaustive search about the matter came to naught. She suspected that Poh Lin's parents had never bothered to send her to school. But no matter. With or without the three Rs, she would take Poh Lin in. And so Poh Lin joined the School for the Blind as a boarder.

Poh Lin was then a rather mousy girl who kept to herself. But it did not take long for the teachers to take note of her intelligence and willingness to learn. Her ability to surmount her double handicap came to the notice of the Royal Commonwealth Society for the Blind in Britain and before long, experts from overseas were in Singapore to test and assess Chan Poh Lin. They were enthusiastic and excited that she had the potential for more advanced formal education. They envisioned her as the Helen Keller[1] of the East, no less.

For Poh Lin, her nightmare had become a wonderful dream

come true. She was on her way to the Perkins School for the Blind in Boston, Massachusetts, on scholarship! A multiple-handicapped girl from the slums of Singapore was off to the United States of America, the very first from Singapore, possibly of the region, to study and train at the world-renowned centre. Sir John Wilson of the British Royal Commonwealth Society of the Blind and Mr Edward J. Waterhouse of the Perkins School played crucial roles in getting her to Perkins. Mr Waterhouse, then a director of Perkins, flew to Singapore to check what he had already been told: Poh Lin's potential for "better education". At that time, he could not communicate well with Poh Lin but Mrs Choy was there to bridge the communication gap.

Poh Lin would remain at Perkins for a total of eleven years. Each year, there would be airline tickets for her and a full-time companion to spend the summer vacation in Singapore. Each year, the decision rested with Poh Lin whether it should be a one-way or two-way trip. "In 1971, she chose home." Mr Waterhouse emphasised that it was her choice. She had graduated from Perkins; she had received and completed high school – her "formal education". To advance to the tertiary level would be out of the question without financial assistance; it was only available if she took up American citizenship. Poh Lin opted to return to Singapore for good.

The diffident teenager who left Singapore in 1960 hanging on to the arm of her specially-selected companion for the distant unknown, returned to Singapore eleven years later an educated adult, brimming with life and self-confidence. There was the offer of a job, from the very school which she once attended. She started work as a proof-reader. When there was a teaching post vacant, she became an arts and craft teacher. Although she had not been trained to teach, she seemed happy to do her part in the school in Toa Payoh Rise, renamed the Singapore School for the Visually Handicapped.

On the home-front, the slums of Sago Lane had been demolished and the Chans resettled on the top floor – the penthouse floor – of a block of high-rise public housing that offered cross ventilation and a panoramic view of Chinatown. Although the address was still Sago Lane, the airy, two-bedroom flat was worlds apart from the fetid cubicle the Chans once occupied. Poh Lin's father having died, she lived with her mother until the latter's death in the early 1990s. Poh Lin the fastidious housekeeper – a trait that first became evident soon after her exposure to the western ways at Perkins – would make sure that the sparsely but adequately furnished flat was never short of being spotless and dust-free. She was meticulous in her dressing and careful about her weight – and therefore diet-conscious. After the death of her mother, Poh Lin lived in the flat alone, quite able to look after her own daily needs, from cooking to laundry to cleaning the refrigerator and mopping the floor.

Mrs Choy had kept in touch with Poh Lin and her progress at Perkins. By the time Poh Lin returned to Singapore to live and work, Mrs Choy had long left the School of the Blind and returned to teaching at St Andrew's. But whatever her other commitments, she made time for Poh Lin and her mother. The latter's health had been failing for some years before her death; Mrs Choy would often be the one to accompany her to the doctors and help her with the family's marketing.

It was in the early 1980s when the three-storey YMCA building at One Orchard Road – where Mrs Choy spent the worst days and nights of her life as a prisoner of the Japanese occupation forces forty years earlier – was completely demolished and rebuilt. Only then did she find it bearable to be in its vicinity, and even to enter the premises, all of nine storeys, complete with a roof-top swimming pool. (She recalled that the first time she entered the new structure was to attend a meeting concerning senior citizens.) Ever on the look-out to make life easier and happier for others, in this case, Poh Lin, it occurred to her that perhaps she could obtain permission for Poh Lin to make use of the pool. Approval was promptly forthcoming from the management of the YMCA.

However, despite her admirable ability to do many things on her own, Poh Lin was still dependent on the sighted to get about. Mrs Choy found that getting permission to use the swimming pool was the easy part, finding someone willing to accompany Poh Lin was a most daunting search. The volunteer would have to fetch Poh Lin from her flat in Sago Lane, escort her to the YMCA in Orchard Road, wait for her to have her swim, then send her home. Occasionally, there was the odd inquiry or even offer, especially when Poh Lin or Mrs Choy had been in the news. For a decade from the mid-1980s, there was just one volunteer who actually took over the weekly ritual. Understandably, there were communication problems with Poh Lin. In addition, her companion or escort of the day would be embarrassed as Poh Lin tended to be loud and brusque.

On her swimming days, the escort would often be asked by Poh Lin to take a minor detour to the wet market in Chinatown. Once there, Poh Lin would choose for herself whatever she needed to buy. If it were fruit, she would pick up each one and not only feel but press. That inevitably led to protests from the vendors; this in turn upset whoever that was with Poh Lin. Mrs Choy, fully aware of the way Poh Lin did her marketing, was unfazed. How was Poh Lin to tell if she did not touch? And being able to choose was part of her independence. When Poh Lin spoke, it sounded like growls, causing those within hearing to turn and stare. But Mrs Choy never discouraged Poh Lin from speaking – whatever the reaction it brought.

There were occasions when Mrs Choy faced conflicting demands on her time on Poh Lin's swimming days. One instance was when Mrs Choy's Indonesian maid took long leave and there was no one available to baby-sit Mrs Choy's granddaughter who lived with her. She wanted dearly to stay at home and look after the infant but she had her appointment with Poh Lin to keep. It was not possible to cancel or change the appointment. Poh Lin had no telephone in her flat – what would the deaf do with a telephone? Sending a messenger – if she could find one – would also be futile. Poh Lin would not be able to hear the knock on the door. There was no use slipping a note under the door for the blind. Appointments with Poh Lin were thus always rigidly fixed in advance. Just about the only occasion Mrs Choy failed to keep an appointment with Poh Lin was the day her husband died suddenly on 2 October 1985.

For Mrs Choy, the sign language she learnt in prison became useful to communicate with Poh Lin. With the deaf and blind, the same set of signs becomes the touch method. When Poh Lin needed to communicate with Mrs Choy, she also resorted to the manual typewriter whose keyboard she mastered, along with that of the Braille machine. If what was on her mind could be simply expressed or if she wanted to respond spontaneously, she used her voice. When Mrs Choy first started taking Poh Lin for her swim, it was a weekly ritual which involved accompanying her to the bank, to the wet market and provision shops as well as to the hairdresser. Poh Lin would have typed out a list of the things she would like done on each of Mrs Choy's visits, often embellishing her missive with her thoughts of the moment, mostly on people she and Mrs Choy knew. Each outing ended with lunch, usually in a food centre in the Sago Lane area.

Some months after Mrs Choy's eighty-third birthday, Poh Lin told her that henceforth she would be content with just a fortnightly swim. Much had happened in the intervening years to strain the singularly remarkable relationship between the two. Few, if any, could understand why and how Mrs Choy would continue to put aside time specially for Poh Lin. (Some conjecture that perhaps Poh Lin was veteran social worker Mrs Choy's *raison d'etre* in her twilight years.) At an age when her contemporaries were either complaining copiously of arthritic pains and other assorted geriatric ailments and generally demanding to be pampered by family-members, and enjoying themselves as indulgent grandparents (or perhaps great grandparents) – Mrs Choy shouldered quite alone a responsibility that should surely not fall on her, in giving her helping hand, and more, to Poh Lin.

In 1990 Poh Lin's services were terminated by the School for the Visually Handicapped. By then, despite her lack of formal training as a teacher, she had chalked up nineteen years of service. Whether she had prior warning from the school management that her performance as a teacher was not up to the mark, or whether it had deteriorated over the years – it was understandably a great shock to Poh Lin. It was also a great shock to Mrs Choy who found it bewildering that Poh Lin could have done so badly as a teacher that she deserved the ultimate judgement. She energetically came to Poh Lin's defence. She tried to dissuade the school from enforcing the termination; she tried to persuade the administration to allow Poh Lin – then forty-five years old – to stay on in some other post, perhaps a non-teaching one, till she reached retirement age. When it became plain that the management was adamant in acting on its decision to discharge Poh Lin without further ado, Mrs Choy tried to obtain a better financial settlement for her.

In the meantime, she successfully placed Poh Lin and her mother on social welfare. Her friends rallied to her appeal; there were cash donations from several of them while others bought provisions for Poh Lin and her mother. Among the most generous must surely be Mrs Choy's long-time friend, Mrs Constance Goh Sai-Poh, Singapore's family planning pioneer. The two women were fellow warriors in the battle against unwanted babies in those fledgling days of the movement after the Second World War and had kept in touch. Mrs Goh, renowned for her generosity, had earlier paid for Poh Lin's costly hearing aids. When she heard of Poh Lin's financial worries, she not only gave cash but, for many years, also sent Poh Lin monthly cheques plus bonuses for Christmas and Lunar New Year.

When news of Poh Lin's termination reached the press, journalists sought Mrs Choy out for clarification over the dismissal. Mrs Choy did what she could to brief the press on the unfortunate situation, blaming neither party. Someone read the press report to Poh Lin. She was infuriated. She accused Mrs Choy of taking sides, of betraying her. She conveyed her thoughts via her manual typewriter, revealing an astonishing ease with and command of gutter diction. She told Mrs Choy in no uncertain terms: "From now on, I do not want to go out with you; I do not want your help; I do not want you to talk on my behalf...."

Word also got round that Poh Lin had been violent with Mrs Choy, slapping her in public. Mrs Choy made light of it all and brushed aside the slapping incident as "nothing in it, she didn't mean to hurt me." She even came up with several explanations for Poh Lin's action. (One explanation: Slapping, to Poh Lin, is "a form of endearment." Another: "The Chinese are prone to slapping each other.") She steadfastly attempted to rationalise away Poh Lin's behaviour in the aftermath of her loss of job. At the same time, she made it plain to Poh Lin that she would always be there for her, no matter what.

One can understand and indeed, sympathise with Poh Lin's anger over her summary dismissal, but surely not her treatment of Mrs Choy. She had lashed out at the one person who stood by her through the years, the one person who went out of her way to protect her. Mrs Choy was not blind to the facts before her for she understood Poh Lin more than anyone else, probably better than Poh Lin herself. Poh Lin, she explained, was bitter and hurt. She felt that people had let her down. With her formal education from Perkins, she had possibly expected recognition and status. Those who had helped her did not expect her conquest of her disabilities to stop with her graduation from Perkins. They had ambitions for her. They looked forward to her further progress as an illustrious example in the East, as the author of at least one book, her autobiography. Poh Lin was sorely disappointed that this had not been so.

No matter how disrespectful and presumptuous Poh Lin was, Mrs Choy continued to board a bus in Bukit Timah Road every other Wednesday morning, getting off in New Bridge Road, and walked to the block of flats where Poh Lin lived to accompany her to the YMCA for her swim – thereafter, to run the errands Poh Lin had planned for the day. Sometimes, the chores come first, then the swim. Or the swim could be sandwiched in between chores. Each outing took up about five hours. Mrs Choy was reluctant to admit that Poh Lin could be difficult but she did admit that before leaving her home to meet Poh Lin she would say a silent prayer.

When Mrs Choy sat in the shade[2] by the pool while Poh Lin swam, one recurring thought bothered her. Once, she pensively wondered aloud if she had done Poh Lin a great disservice by encouraging her to take up the scholarship offered by Perkins. At that time, it seemed like a sublime gift to Poh Lin, to be given a golden opportunity to open up her mind, to reach her full intellectual potential, and later, to inspire others with her achievements as a disabled person.

Perhaps she should just have left her in Sago Lane, and not persevered in persuading her parents first, to send her to the School for the Blind and later, to give their consent for her to go overseas. If one thing had not led to the other, Poh Lin would not have become a teacher at the school in Toa Payoh Rise and be subject to the anguish and humiliation of dismissal. But there was no turning back the clock. She had opened the door to a new life for Poh Lin and she felt it was her responsibility to continue nurturing that life.

Now and again, Mrs Choy cast her eyes in the direction of the pool where Poh Lin swam ever so confidently. When she was not doing breaststroke or backstroke or just floating lazily on her back, she stood chest-deep, swinging and stretching her arms above the water rhythmically while lifting her face skywards, as if the better to absorb the rays of the sun.

To Mrs Choy, Poh Lin was forever her "poor dear", and she could not bring herself to deny Poh Lin the simple pleasure of being in the water. Looking at the tanned woman in the YMCA's roof-top pool, she smiled and gently said: "When she is in the pool, it is about the only time when I see her so radiantly happy. How can I deny her that?"

---

1   Helen Adams Keller (1880-1968) of the United States of America overcame her deafness and blindness to graduate from the prestigious Radcliffe College *cum laude*; among the specialised institutions that contributed to her triumph over her handicaps and helped her to acquire speech was the Perkins School for the Blind in Boston, Massachusetts. She wrote several books; among them were her widely-read autobiographies.

2   She would usually spend the time reading or writing letters. Most of the interviews for this biography were done on the rooftop of the YMCA.

XIII

THE HOUSE OF CHOY

THIRTY YEARS LATE. But he made it. In 1946, Choy Khun Heng did not go when the Red Cross invited him and his wife to Britain to recuperate from the ordeals they had suffered during the Japanese occupation. When he finally went to England in 1976, it was, to him, almost like a pilgrimage. Although he was by nature a home-body who did not rate travelling a particularly pleasurable pastime, visiting Britain was something he had promised himself, his family and his friends in that far-flung country. That day finally came when he retired from the Borneo Company in 1976. He was certainly no job-hopper, having served that one organisation all his working life, spanning well over four decades, with a war wedged in between. By then, his wife too had finally retired, at the end of 1974 from St Andrew's Junior School. This time, they travelled together to Britain.

Eldest daughter Bridget was then in Britain where she had studied chartered accountancy. She had extended her stay to work and gain experience in her profession. Bridget was only too happy to arrange for her parents to have a leisurely and carefree summer, sightseeing and visiting friends in Britain and touring Europe. It was planned that the three of them would return to Singapore together, just in time to attend the Choys' youngest daughter Irene's October wedding. It would be the first wedding in the Choy family. All went idyllically for a while. They spent time in Scotland and Wales. Tickets were booked for a tour of Europe. They were still in Britain – in Birmingham – when diabetes got the better of Mr Choy. Instead of crossing the channel, he had to be hospitalised forthwith.

It came to the notice of the hospital staff that the patient was an Officer of the Order of the British Empire – they had spotted the burn scars on his legs and the letters *OBE* engraved on the back of his watch, a retirement gift from the Borneo Company. That was all the hospital needed. He was given first-class care, free of charge throughout the several months he was hospitalised. Although the hospital was not ready to discharge the patient, he was restive and wanted to return home to Singapore. The Choys took an Aeroflot flight home. Despite its price competitiveness, the airline was not the travelling public's popular choice, for which Mrs Choy was very glad indeed. It meant that there were lots of empty seats and her husband could stretch out comfortably throughout the long journey home. But they had missed Irene's wedding.

Once back in Singapore, it was back to hospital again for Mr Choy. In retrospect, Mrs Choy reckoned that it was fortuitous indeed that her husband had fallen seriously ill in Britain where he was given such superb medical care. The quality care gave him an extra lease of life. He died nine years later of a heart attack, aged seventy-six.

To people who knew him, the Hongkong-born Mr Choy was a kindly person, infinitely patient and accommodating. He must indeed have had patience in abundance for he waited nearly a decade for Elizabeth Yong Su-Moi to become his wife. He must surely also have had an extraordinary inner reserve of resilience and strength that might not have been apparent to the casual acquaintance. How else could he have withstood the brutal treatment meted out to him by the Japanese during those nightmarish weeks, months and years in the hands of the *Kempeitai*? (Physical abuse aside, the malnourishment resulted in beri-beri. The scars – visible and hidden – of the physical abuse inflicted on him remained for the rest of his life.) In the post-war years, especially during the 1950s when Mrs Choy's balancing act as a teacher cum legislator cum social worker cum homemaker was stretched to the limit, he was the man behind the woman, the anchor at home.

It was just as well too that his widowed sister, Madam Choy Yuet Kum, had moved in with them; she became the much needed stabiliser at home for the children. To them, there was always *gu-ma* (father's older sister) to turn to. The children had arrived between 1950 and 1954, during Mrs Choy's Legislative Council years. The years also covered her three-month lecture tour of North America and her five-week trip to London to represent Singapore at the Coronation of Queen Elizabeth II. Between 1950 and 1955, she also took part in two elections. All that time, she was teaching at St Andrew's while the three little girls were growing and in need of attention and nurture. It was just as well that Bridget, Lynette and Irene were obedient children who did not require stringent supervision and who were never – well, almost never – in need of stern discipline.

In Bridget's memory, she and her sisters were "born good"; they never gave their parents cause to be upset with them. Hence, there was no call for reprimand or punishment because they always behaved exemplarily.

As far as Mrs Choy was concerned, they were her and her husband's lovable daughters. No favourites. Each one was precious and special. (The daughters' collective memories differ. But all are agreed that *gu-ma* had been Irene's protector.) Mrs Choy the mother was determined to give the girls the best she and her husband could afford. As with many parents, she wanted her children to have all that she had once longed for but could not have, like tertiary education, or the ability to play musical instruments. The Choys were salary earners and were by no means wealthy – Mrs Choy was a primary school teacher and her husband had started out as a bookkeeper, later promoted to the rank of accountant. But they would not deny their children what they as parents considered

Mrs Choy communicating with
Theresa Chan Poh Lin who is deaf,
mute and blind, circa 1957.

ABOVE Greece, 1958.

RIGHT Elizabeth and her sisters
Annie (middle) and Doris, 1965.

ABOVE The Choy family,
Christmas, 1971.

LEFT Mrs Choy, 1968, aged 58.

LEFT   Mrs Choy with her last but one class at St. Andrew's Junior School. When she retired in 1974, she had served the school for all of 35 years.

LEFT   Portrait of Mrs Choy attached to the correspondence with the lady-in-waiting of Queen Elizabeth II in 1989.

RIGHT   Mrs Choy's notes on her delightful gift of two jade chicks to Queen Elizabeth II, Prince Philip and the Queen Mother, 10 October 1989.

BOTTOM   Po-po with Stefanie, November 1989.

To Your Majesty + His Royal Highness,
Greetings + welcome to Singapore.
May your stay be a happy one.
Please accept this small gift of
2 jade chicks as a souvenir from
Singapore. Perhaps they will amuse
your grand-children.
Thank you for coming to visit
our country. We love + admire you.
With best wishes + respect. Elizabeth Choy
10·10·89.

10·10·89. Singapore.
To Your Majesty The Queen Mother,
Greetings to you Ma'am. Please accept
this small gift of 2 jade chicks as a
souvenir from Singapore. I well remember
our meeting on 25·7·46 — just your
Majesty and myself at Buckingham Palace
I remember how your Kindness, concern
and graciousness moved me to tears.
Perhaps the two little chicks will amuse
your Majesty's great-grand-children.
With love + best wishes From Elizabeth Choy.

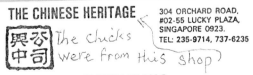

THE CHINESE HERITAGE

304 ORCHARD ROAD,
#02-55 LUCKY PLAZA,
SINGAPORE 0923.
TEL: 235-9714, 737-6235

The chicks were from this shop

DAVID WANG

2ND LEVEL (NEXT TO SONY CONSUMER SERVICE CENTER)

Recommended by Singapore Tourist Promotion Board
Blackwood Furniture, Fine Arts, Antiques, Valuers, Insurance

BELOW Family portrait taken in the Choy's Mackenzie Road home on Mrs Choy's 84th birthday. Back row, from left: Bridget's husband Bay Heng Tai, Bridget, Lynette, Irene's husband Michael Ong, Irene, Lynette's husband Vincent Wong. Seated with their grandmother were, from left: Cheryl Ong, Stefanie Bay, Andrea Wong and Colin Ong.

ABOVE Mrs Choy's 91st birthday, 2001. Back row, from left: Lynette's husband Vincent Wong, grandchildren Cheryl Ong and Colin Ong, Irene's husband Michael Ong, granddaughter Stefanie Bay. Seated with Mrs Choy from left: Irene, Lynette, Bridget and Bridget's husband Bay Heng Tai.

OVERLEAF Portrait of Mrs Choy in the bedroom of her Mackenzie Road home by Ung Ruey Loon, March 2005.

important to each child's total development. In retrospect, the three grown daughters are very aware of the amount of self-denial on the part of their parents.

The Choys were not afraid of letting their daughters know that they were not their natural parents. In the case of Bridget, as far back as she could recall, her adoptive mother would take her to visit her natural parents and meet her siblings. But she assumed that her mother, Mrs Choy, had taken her to visit her friends where there were young children to play with her. There came a time when Bridget was getting rather confused and sought answers from her parents. For example, during those visits, she overheard comments about her physical resemblance to the other children; then there was the reference to her as sister. How could that be? The Choys decided it was time for her to know. Bridget was then about ten years old. They explained how she came to be their eldest daughter, emphasizing that it was very painful for her natural parents to have to give her up for adoption. Although Bridget had known for some time that Lynette and Irene were adopted, she assumed that she was not. Thus, she was stunned to learn the truth. It took her several days to absorb the fact, to understand and accept reality. Once that was over, she continued to visit her natural parents and meet her natural siblings regularly, especially on festivals.

For Lynette, she learnt of her other family when she was about seven years old. By then, the Choys had lost touch with Lynette's natural parents. "I used to ask my parents (the Choys), where did I come from?" recalled Lynette. It was not so much out of a sense of insecurity as a child's innocent expression of curiosity concerning her other family. Much later, she learnt that because Mrs Choy was often in the public eye, it had been easy for her other family to keep track of her. At the age of seventeen, a go-between approached Lynette, letting her know that her natural parents would like to meet her. Lynette sought approval of the Choys before meeting them. Since then, she has kept in touch with her other family. (Her natural parents had one more child after Lynette.) It was perhaps unfortunate that before the Choys could explain to Irene, a relative told the little girl about her natural parents. It was a rather devastating revelation to the primary school child.

Lynette is objective. She sees and appreciates her adoptive parents' magnanimity. She is aware that not many would care to share their adopted children with their natural parents. In the case of the Choys, not only did they let the children know, they openly encouraged each child to know their other family better. They also took pains to reassure each child that she was not an unwanted and unloved child to her natural parents; rather, it was because the natural parents loved the child that they gave her up for adoption, knowing she would have a better life with foster parents. As one eminently qualified to speak, Bridget's advice to foster parents is to let the children know as early as possible.

In every way, the Choys showed the girls how much they cared for them. Thus, the parents would make sure the three girls had their meals first, had the choicest pieces of every dish, before they sat down to eat. If transport was needed, Mrs Choy would be available as chauffeur. When she waited for the girls to have their music lessons or tuition, she would read, study or write. (Not having a proper table-top to write on never deterred her.) At one stage, Lynette recalled her mother spending the time while she had her piano lesson studying Malay in the car. To Lynette, an unforgettable characteristic of her mother's personality was that she was never idle.

All three girls attended St Margaret's School. The school was chosen not only because it is an Anglican school, but also because its primary school is within walking distance from their Mackenzie Road home. Mackenzie Road skirts the foot of Mount Emily. One can easily take a short cut up the hill and reach the school. The girls did not fail their parents in their studies. (When deemed necessary, tuition would be arranged to see each one through a hurdle – like for Chinese.) Bridget left to further her studies in accountancy in Britain.[1] Lynette took her Bachelor of Arts in Singapore, then proceeded to Australia for a post-grad Library studies course. Irene too obtained academic qualification, also in accountancy – from the then University of Singapore. After a spell in an accounting firm, she ran a kindergarten.

As a child, Mrs Choy's love of music had to be put aside. Thus, she made sure her three daughters received music lessons from young, whatever the cost. Her husband, a music lover who played the violin, was all for instilling music appreciation in their children. It thrilled the Choys to watch the girls develop their musicianship and mastery of the keyboard. But perhaps the parents had, like so many doting parents, neglected to ascertain the children's own interests. The two older girls refrained from saying anything about music lessons that might upset their parents for they knew how much they wanted them to learn music; they were also aware the music lessons cost a lot of money. They might also have known that their music teacher, reputedly one of the best in Singapore, charged fees commensurate with her standing in the music circle. Bridget and Lynette persevered and each completed the grade eight of the Royal School of Music of Britain. It was perhaps regrettable that they should have had to suffer to reach there.

It had to do with the music teacher. Typical of many, she was examination oriented. Perhaps her standing in the music world was directly related to the number of distinctions awarded to those groomed by her. It was clear that she wanted her students to consistently sparkle in the annual examinations. Often, during lesson time, to get her point across, she would grip the students' arms. Bridget and Lynette both had bruises aplenty to show for it. Their father was quite upset at the sight of the blue-black marks, so too their *gu-ma*, but their mother seemed to make light of the evidence. She assumed the girls had not practised enough, thus annoying the teacher. Hence, her response was to urge them to practise harder. To the girls, it was not just the bruises; much worse was the scolding and haranguing that rendered piano lessons a torture. In retrospect, they should have made their distress known to the grown-ups at home, but they did not. They should have requested for a change of teacher, but they did not.

Bridget and Lynette both shudder when recalling their dreaded piano lessons. They would literally make Bridget break out in cold sweat. Lynette remembers that her lessons were on Mondays and her weekends would therefore be spent in great anxiety. The trauma was such that Lynette, once praised by the teacher as "very musical," did not touch the keyboard for a few years after she passed her grade eight. Thus, when her only child, a daughter, wanted to give up piano lessons at the intermediate level, she had no objection.

The more outspoken and strong-willed Irene had a better time. She decided unilaterally to quit after the third grade. It was not because of her teacher; the teacher who taught the lower grades was a rather easy-going, kindly woman. Irene just did not like classical music. Her father remonstrated; he urged that she should at least learn to play one instrument. Since she did not like classical music, he suggested a switch to jazz. Irene did not really know what jazz was; but it sounded like it was not classical music and that would do. Without further ado, she happily switched to another teacher who taught her jazz pieces on the piano. Along the way, she also picked up the guitar. For her, music has been fun.

For many years, the House of Choy resembled a refugee camp. By default, it was left to *gu-ma* to enforce some semblance of order in the rather chaotic household. There were always so many people in the homestead. At the bare minimum, there would be eight: The parents and the three girls, *gu-ma* and two live-in maids. But in any average week, the population would be more than that. Mrs Choy's inability to say no to requests for help had of course much to do with the appearance of strangers not only at the meal table but in their bedrooms as well. It did not matter that there were just four bedrooms. "The floor is of wood; mats would do." In addition, that is, to all the double-decker beds. Hers was dubbed the 'elastic house' which expanded when the need arose.

Apart from the people who at one time or other sponged off the Choys, there were the others brought home by Mrs Choy – the social worker – who lived up to her motto: "My home is your home." There were the victims of fires and floods. In such cases, it would mean accommodating whole families. Then there were the children. Lynette remembers the polio victims her mother brought home. One was a Malay girl; Lynette would watch her mother picking lice from the girl's hair. Another was an Indian girl who stayed for some time. There was also a Eurasian girl with an angelic face but sadly, she had a brain tumour. Mrs Choy would at times host the ill and/or disabled from beyond the shores of Singapore. For example, in 1957-1958, she hosted a crippled girl from Sarawak when the child came to receive orthopaedic treatment in Singapore. Upon successful completion of her treatment, it was Mrs Choy who accompanied her back to Sarawak.

There were the blind children from the School for the Blind. But these were mostly day visitors. Mrs Choy would bring a few of them at a time to join family outings (to the beach, for instance) and family functions (birthday and Christmas parties). Even after she had left the school, blind children would come a-calling.[2] The Choy girls also met Chan Poh Lin. Mrs Choy would bring Poh Lin to Mackenzie Road when she was back in Singapore during her Perkins' school breaks. Lynette learnt to communicate with Poh Lin quite well, using the touch method. Poh Lin would entertain Lynette and keep the younger girl enthralled with tales of life at Perkins and her adventures in the United States of America. In the late 1960s, the Mackenzie Road terrace house had a Christmas Island invasion. There was a bevy of girls from that island, in Singapore to study, with nowhere to stay. Who else could they turn to but to Mrs Choy?

It was just as well that both her husband and sister-in-law were also kind and accommodating people. But there were doubtless times when they would have fervently wished that Mrs Choy would learn to say no and be more discerning in extending help to others. To her accountant husband, his wife's carelessness with money must surely have caused him considerable anxiety, bearing in mind that there were the three children who had come to them relatively late in life. However, whatever friction there might have been between husband and wife, they did their utmost to keep it from the girls. Perhaps being introverted, Lynette was specially sensitive. As a young child, she did not understand the words uttered but she could sense tension in the voices of her parents.

"Somehow, each time I heard my parents argue, I always thought it was my fault," recalls the soft-spoken Lynette. According to Mrs Choy, she and her husband were too busy to have time to disagree or quarrel. But Lynette does remember quite clearly one incident involving her when her mother became quite angry with her father. Lynette's father had refused to allow her to go out with a group of young friends because there were boys in the group. Lynette was already in her mid-teens but the protective father became very obdurate over his veto. His more liberated wife felt that Lynette was old enough – and sensible enough – to take care of herself. She made her opinion known to her husband quite heatedly.

The Choys did their parenting with gusto, especially when the girls were young. Outside of work commitments, their lives were planned round the children, to give the girls as much enjoyment and happiness as they could. Childhood, the Choys firmly believed, should not be just lessons and examinations. There were the weekend treats, usually to one of the amusement parks. There were the 'worlds' of Singapore: Gay World, Great World, Happy World and New World. These were the entertainment centres for families, with something for everyone. Within each world, there were cabarets and cinemas; there were shops aplenty, selling dresses, shoes, provisions, herbs, and there were photo studios too. For the children, there would be the playgrounds offering joy rides, including the Ferris wheel to excite and thrill, or, for the more faint-hearted, the merry-go-round. Within each amusement park there would of course be the ubiquitous food stalls and restaurants.

Mr Choy loved eating-several bowls of his favourite noodles at one sitting; thirty sticks of satay at one go. (Perhaps he was making up for the deprivation during the war.) It was no wonder that his girth grew bigger and rounder by the year. There would also be visits to a relative's farm in Choa Chu Kang. The children were allowed to roam freely and pluck any fruit they fancied within the orchard or play with the ducks and chicks and whatever other fowl and animals there were. To Mrs Choy, it was just a faint reminder of life in the Borneon wilds. Then there were the trips to St John's Island where they had access to a bungalow. The whole family – probably extended to relatives and friends – would get there by ferry to spend perhaps a week of the school vacation.

For the children, one of the most memorable and thrilling bits of their childhood was riding in their mother's car. (How their mother learnt to drive is a story in itself. Mrs Choy would say she never needed to learn how to drive; she just got behind the steering wheel of a car and drove off. But that's not quite the whole truth. Her brother Chau Vui – victim of Japanese mopping up in 1942 when he was seventeen years old – taught his older siblings how to drive when he was just twelve.) The car that everyone remembers most fondly was a boneshaker, a tiny little Fiat, a two-door tin-can in faded green, with a collapsible hood. Mrs Choy took special pride in this jalopy. With the hood down, she had natural ventilation – wind in her face and hair.

She would challenge anyone who dared to belittle her vehicle. She proved the versatility of her car again and again. The little auto, with hood down, could ferry no less than fifteen persons, big and small (mostly small). That was how the children travelled to Changi beach, with the riders at the back either standing or kneeling on the seats throughout the breezy journey. She would drive this same same jalopy – doubtless an eye sore to some – to Legislative Council meetings. Parking was so easy; she would nonchalantly squeeze it in between the gleaming Jaguars, Rovers, Bentleys and Rolls Royces.

1   It was in the late 1960s when Bridget left to further her studies in Britain. The mindful Choys, careful that their daughters should never have cause to doubt their policy of treating all three girls equally, took the two younger girls for a holiday in Cambodia. This was their way of reassuring them that there was no favouritism involved in sending Bridget overseas.

2   During the years when Mrs Choy was the principal of the School for the Blind, she was provided with a flat within the school compound and was expected to live there. There were occasions when there was a reverse flow in human traffic when the daughters would spend weekends at their mother's flat in the school.

XIV
UNDAUNTED & INSATIATED

ELIZABETH CHOY'S FREINDS and acquaintances – especially those of the Hakka community – jestfully referred to her as the 'Dayak woman of Singapore'.

Of course, the choice of description revealed ignorance on the part of the originator of the nickname: Dayaks are generally associated more with Sarawak while Mrs Choy hailed from Sabah, where the Kadazans have for long had numerical superiority. Dayak or Kadazan, one could quite easily conjecture the source of inspiration. She was large-framed, bigger built than the average Singapore woman. Her complexion was rather dark, darker than the average ethnic Chinese. Then there was her hairstyle – she often favoured a short fringe, worn arguably most famously by Temenggong Jugah of Sarawak, a direct descendant of Dayak head-hunters, he who became Federal Minister of Sarawak Affairs when Malaysia came into existence in 1963. And of course the finishing touches to her dressing – a flower in her hair and often, the fine, handbraided bracelets made by the Kadazans from bracken fern; she had dozens of these on her left wrist. All these elements added up and made her look different. Members of the Hakka community in Singapore were not interested in being accurate; to them, she was how they pictured a Dayak woman.

Through the years, the changes in her were more cosmetic than real. Signs of age were clearly visible. While her face remained remarkably unlined, there was a generous spread of age spots; her thick, black hair thinned markedly and became variegated shades of grey; just as visible was a broadening of her girth. For decades, she had strictly – and successfully – kept her weight capped at fifty-five kilogrammes until aging dictated otherwise.

But little really changed in Mrs Choy's distinctive personality and character even as she grew older. She was always strikingly contradictory and remained consistently so. The failings of others did not diminish her kind-heartedness and generosity. In contrast, she was impetuous and thrifty. There were always laudable – to her, altruistic – explanatiosn for what she did, but because she often charged forth into action without pausing to consider the likely repercussions on and reactions of people involved, the results of her impulsive deeds at times brought, to her consternation and chagrin, negative reactions.

Her thrift was legendary; indeed, seen to have been excessive. But again there were contradictions. On the one hand, there are those who remember her as the fancy dresser; but there was the other side of her, one who thought nothing of wearing hand-me-downs, or of bestowing a new lease of life on discarded goods. She had, for example, used her eldest daughter's well-worn purse for years – with dozens of rubber-bands to reinforce the catch – and refused to part with it. To her, taxis were an unjustifiable expense if the bus service covered the destination she wished to go to; she even gave buses a miss if the destination was within walking distance. And she would rather go home for a meal than spend $2 on a plate of noodles or rice in a hawker centre because the meal at home, in her estimation, cost less. This was the same person who did not hesitate to give away her own money (or things, often new) to others whom she perceived to be in need. This same person was the darling of tour guides during an early-1995 vacation in China because she carefreely gave tips of S$50 to S$100 to each guide –

over and above the mandatory charge pre-collected by the travel agency.

Her interpretation of family values and obligations revealed unconventional thoughts and convictions. If she was conservative, it should surprise no one, considering her family background, her vintage and her extensive exposure to the 'missionary way' during her formative years. Despite her English education and religion, she believed strongly in Chinese family traditions and values, especially in filial piety. Her own interpretation of the latter was an unquestioning acceptance of her responsibility as the eldest of her parents' children. By so doing, she seemed to have swept aside the traditional Chinese emphasis on the eldest *male* child. Her unilateral commitment to be her younger siblings' surrogate parent and provider seemed openended. Thus, her devotion to her siblings appeared undiluted even after her marriage.

Her attitude towards marriage – at least of her own – was enigmatic. It was neither an old-fashioned match-made betrothal nor a modern marriage born of mutual attraction and love. By her own admission, she had no enthusiasm for marriage when her future mother-in-law broached the subject, but had consented to it, as she rationalised, because it would be in keeping with her 'missionary upbringing'. Mrs Choy, by deed rather than by slogan, was a front-runner of the feminist movement and Confucius, whose words of wisdom she learnt from her father and often quoted, would doubtless have turned in his grave. Other than dutifully adopting the surname Choy as hers, marriage did not seem to alter an iota of her perceived familial obligations to her siblings; nor did it curb her freedom and independence to pursue whatever interests that drew her. In her first decade of marriage – by fate (her husband's incarceration, followed by hers) and design (the fact that a six-month stay in Britain stretched to a full four years) – the amount of time she spent with her husband could best be counted in months.

The liberated and enlightened aspect of her character was admirably obvious in her acceptance of adoption as a means to parenthood; so too her lack of gender bias in approaching adoption.

In her role as a mother, she displayed the typical devotion of a traditional parent who would deny herself materially so that she could lavish on the children. In retrospect, in all likelihood, it was the children who made the household a family. Husband and wife found common interest in the children. They were both selflessly devoted and dedicated to the nurturing of their three girls. Mrs Choy took pains to instill in her daughters the values she respected and treasured, among them, filial piety as she understood it.

Nevertheless, to Mrs Choy, the affection she received from her daughters – "they are the most filial of daughters" – and her own ability and capacity to enjoy life were far more important than any material concern. She often jokingly admitted to being the poorest member of her family. "Everyone else has mansions and big cars. I've nothing. My relatives ask me what happened. They say: You are cleverer than anyone else in the family; you work harder than anyone else; you are thriftier than anyone else – so what happened?" Her inability to protect her personal properties, as evinced by her repeated encounters with the deceitful and the confidence tricksters, is on record. Compounding this was her unhesitant selfless giving of cash and kind.

She was also denied what should surely be rightfully hers. She was unable to obtain a single cent in war compensation, despite her loss of employment during the war years and the extensive damage to, and looting of, the house she lived in. It seemed that she had been tardy in submitting her claims. She recalled that when the Allied forces first landed in 1945, the soldiers brought with them for free distribution articles of everyday use that had become hard to find and therefore much sought-after during the occupation years. But she did not get anything: "Not even a cake of soap."

When her teaching career that had spanned more than four decades came to a close in 1974, she had yet another unpleasant experience. By then, the government had introduced the thirteenth month pay which teachers were also entitled to. But for Mrs Choy, she was told that because she had retired in November, she was not entitled to the extra month's pay for the year as only those who were on the payroll on 31 December would qualify. She did not choose to retire in November; she was told that her employment would end in November because it was the end of the school year. To her, it was just another of life's trivialities. She admitted to feeling rather upset and even angry over the ruling: "After over forty years teaching, I retired with no pension, no retirement benefits, nothing. Not even a last thirteenth month pay." But she soon shrugged it off: "Rules are rules."

Years later, a former governor of St Andrew's School highlighted the injustice done to her in a letter published in *The Straits Times* on 27 October 1986. Mike Gorrie was writing in response to a press article on Mrs Choy, a sidebar to a preview on a play entitled *Not Afraid To Remember* based on Mrs Choy's war experience. It was he who, as private secretary to the Governor of Singapore, had in 1951 suggested to Governor Sir Franklin Gimson the nomination of Mrs Choy – "one of the most unselfish people I have ever known" – to the Legislative Council. His association with St Andrew's School came later, covering the year Mrs Choy retired. He wrote:

> *I remember how frustrated I was to discover that at the end of her many years of loyal service to the school, she was not considered eligible for a bonus because she was not on the payroll on 31 December, apparently a government requirement. This was not possible because the ministry insisted that she be retired at the end of the school term in November.*

The seeming bureaucratic absurdity was further accentuated when seen against others who benefitted from the ruling.

> *In the same year, my former junior office assistant, an ex-St Andrew's pupil, was doing his National Service. As a punishment for mislaying his rifle, he had his run-out date (ROD) deferred two months, which carried him into January. He told me that he did not mind as it meant he qualified for a bonus.*

Mrs Choy refused to dwell on disappointments, on unpleasant experiences, especially those involving money. They were, for here, mere distractions from the sheer joy of being a teacher.

XV

A CELEBRATED LIFE

AS THE YEARS WENT all too swiftly by, Mrs Choy, the retiree, continued to keep her weeks full. Being elderly and widowed did not lead to a withdrawal from life. (Her husband, Khun Heng, had passed away in 1985.) She remained involved in social work, mainly helping the elderly and the disabled. There were church activities, calling on less mobile family-members, and regular visits to a sister in an old folks home.

And there was always the special slot in her diary for Poh Lin – even when, once, the lift to Poh Lin's twentieth floor flat broke down and Mrs Choy had to climb all the way up, stopping regularly after a few flights of stairs to catch her breath. In 1995, she found a reliable volunteer to bring Poh Lin for her swims. With that settled, she told the helper that she was ready to die. But as the years passed, she joked about how God didn't want her in heaven just yet.

As a mother, she took pride in her daughters, each with her own career and family. The three had, collectively, given her four grandchildren. Youngest daughter Irene, the first to marry, has two children, a boy and a girl. Lynette, who married a year after Irene, has a daughter. (Lynette's wedding in 1977 was the only one of the three daughters' where both parents were present.) Bridget, the eldest, was the last to marry. With the birth of Bridget's daughter Stefanie in 1988, the youngest grandchild occupied centerstage in Mrs Choy's daily routine at home.

But the double-storey terrace house in Mackenzie Road was no longer the fount of seeming madness with its transient residents; it was no longer the destination of the destitute and desperate. The permanent residents too dwindled in number when each daughter moved out of the family nest after marriage.

Elizabeth's thirst for adventure and exposure to new sights and sounds remained insatiated in her old age. Knowing her love for travel, her three daughters included her in their travel plans, be they short excursions across the causeway or visits to countries in the region or further afield. She also did not hesitate to venture forth with other relatives, friends and/or acquaintances.

However, it wasn't the search for adventure that brought her to Kudat, Sabah in 1986. That year, she, her brother Kon Vui and his wife, Maureen, made a long-overdue trip to the land of the siblings' birth – to visit their mother's place of eternal rest. More than half a century had gone by since the death of their mother in 1931. It was an emotionally charged trip down memory lane for Elizabeth and her brother. Time seemed to have stood still in Kudat. The all-engulfing jungle remained defiantly untamed. The walk up to the hill-top to their mother's grave brought back vivid memories of the trekking they did as children.

The year before, the threesome visited the Scandinavian countries. "All the geography lessons I learnt in school came to life there." Just about every country Mrs Choy visited offered its own captivating features, be these wrought by nature or man. As a Christian, Israel was inspirational. That was in 1989: "I couldn't wait to get hold of my Bible to re-read all the stories again. Everything came alive in the Holy Land."

The year before that, in 1988, Mrs Choy made her first trip to China for a totally different but no less enriching and rewarding experience. The twenty-two-day tour was arranged by Bridget who was unable to accompany her mother as she was in an advanced stage of pregnancy. To Su-Moi, the overseas born and bred Chinese, her sojourn in China was an eye-opener. Unlike so many fault-finding, nitpicking tourists from the South Seas, Mrs Choy refused to be distracted by the appalling state of the public facilities, the most infamous being, of course, the lavatories. It was quite immaterial. "China is so big, it's just opened up to tourists. How can we expect the country to get all the facilities ready so fast? We must give it time," she reasoned.

Her reaction to the natural as well as man-made wonders during her tour was perhaps not unlike that of many overseas Chinese visiting the land of their ancestors for the first time. It was an awe-inspiring experience. "It made me proud that I'm Chinese," said Mrs Choy matter-of-factly. That so many historic monuments are Buddhism related did not at all diminish the pleasure she, a Christian, derived as she marvelled at the skill and craft, grit and determination, of a people long gone.

Her verve for more was obvious when she revisited China in early 1995, to experience the sub-zero winter temperature of the north-east of the vast country. Her eagerness to sample unfamiliar cuisine bordered on recklessness. But she contended: "Food is food." The hawker's humble soyabean cake costing just RMB1 a piece was sampled with as much relish as a RMB130 per head fifteen-course *feilong* fusion feast. Fellow tourists gaped as they watched her eagerly go through the courses, with most of the dishes concocted out of every conceivable part of the deer. (An exception was the dessert of snow frogs' fat.) However, much as she enjoyed the food, she was not content with just tasting and savouring local culinary flavours.

She wanted her share of thrills; a horse-cart ride up a treacherous icy track to the mid-level of Jilin's 934-metre Daqing Mountain merely whetted her appetite. She wanted more: such as the twenty-minute ride in a chair-lift to the very top of the mountain – from whence skiers would have a choice of two trails for cross-country skiing. Hearing concerned tourist guides and fellow tourists point out to her that she was surely overaged for such activities did not please her. Her vanity in her own rather amazing physique was also obvious as she defied the elements (despite admitting to a propensity for bronchitis) and repeatedly exposed herself to the sub-zero temperature with inadequate clothing, insisting that it was "not cold" – until a cold caught her. But then needing medical attention in a foreign land was looked upon as a bonus, providing her with an unscheduled experience to cherish. The doctors of a government hospital in Shenyang attended to her before prescribing medication to treat her cough and cold; an electrocardiogram was done, so too X-rays of her chest and a blood test. Total cost: about S$15.

There was more of the world she intended to see – be it Tibet, Turkey or Timbuktu – cataracts notwithstanding. Nor the slight arthritic pressure in her legs she reluctantly admited to. It was uncharacteristic for Elizabeth Choy to ever admit to age being a constraining factor to the lifestyle of her choice. As she had put it: "I want to experience everything; everything."

Yet, that same year of the visit to China, Bridget and her family moved into the Mackenzie Road house with the view to take care of her fiercely independent octogenarian mother.

Mrs Choy was well aware of her aging. She had described herself as a *boh geh* (toothless) old woman but refused to be fitted for dentures. "What for, so old already," she said as a matter of fact. Yet, when she went shopping with her cousins, she would carry the shopping bags although she was the oldest among them.

If Mrs Choy had reflected on her life, she would have recognised that it was what she suffered during the Japanese occupation that defined her to the public. In recognition of her valour during her incarceration and torture, she was awarded the OBE (Order of the British Empire) by the British after the war. She and her husband made history in being the only couple in Singapore to be imprisoned by the Japanese and after the occupation, the only couple to be appointed Officers of the Order of the British Empire for their bravery. From the then Raja of Sarawak, the OSS (Order of the Star of Sarawak), in appreciation of her work as a volunteer nurse before the fall of Singapore; among the civilians she cared for were Sarawakians.

In addition, recognition of her valour during the occupation came from the Girl Guide movement in England. Mrs Choy, a pioneer Girl Guide in British North Borneo in the 1920s, was conferred the Bronze Medal, the movement's highest award.

In 1973, the year before her retirement, came the PBS (Pingkat Bakti Setia) from Singapore. This was an award not related to her wartime exprience but for her long service in education – spread over more than four decades. Earlier, in 1962, there was the Centenary Award from St Andrew's School.

Despite how her war experience had brought media attention – and fame – to Elizabeth Choy Su-Moi, it was, paradoxically, the one topic that she was most reluctant to speak on. The years had failed to numb the pain those memories evoked. Then in 1986, a play based on her experience in the hands of the *Kempaitai* was presented by Theatre Works at the Singapore Drama Festival. Entitled *Not Afraid to Remember*, it was the fruition of director Lim Siauw Chong's[1] persistence and conviction that there was a story worth telling in Mrs Choy's war experience.

Typically, her initial response when approached to sanction the project was a no, followed by a change of heart. While the play received mixed reviews, Mrs Choy was glad that she gave in to her former pupil's persuasion. For her, the play was cathartic – even though the inccessant wailing of a siren at the start of the play caused her to tense up. After watching the play, she found that she no longer froze should anyone broach the subject of the Japanese occupation in her presence; she found that she could talk about it almost impersonally.

Over the years, Elizabeth Choy the war heroine, was featured in books and films. An episode in a series on Singaporean heroes produced by Mediacorp Channel 5 in 2016 dramatised her wartime suffering. In 2017, Sonny Liew, the Eisner-winner comic artist, chose to tell her war story when he was invited to contribute a work for the *Femme Magnifique* graphic novel anthology which features 50 magnificent women including French heroine Joan of Arc and

American abolistionist Harriet Tubman. Of his choice, Liew said, "Her general commitment to public service stood out for me, as did her unwillingness to name her torturers during the War Crime tribunals, placing the onus on war rather than individuals caught up in them." A full-length graphic novel written by Danny Jalil and illustrated by Zaki Ragman, also about her war experiences, was published in 2020. In addition, Mrs Choy had a cameo role as herself in the 2005 Eric Khoo film, *Be With Me*, based on the life of Poh Lin. The scene was of Mrs Choy sitting in a pew some rows behind Poh Lin, watching her pray.

So, while the vicissitudes of war remained a reference point in her life, Elizabeth Choy was content and at peace with herself. This posture was beautifully captured in a portrait by photographer Ung Ruey Loon in 2005 reproduced on the last page of the second plate section of this book. The picture shows Elizabeth Choy sitting serene and poised on her bed. In her signature style, flowers decorate her bun. She is wearing a maroon and black sequined cheongsam – her favourite.

The commission came from the organisers of a charity event called "Breaking the Silence" which promoted awareness of abused women. Mrs Choy was chosen for her "unbreakable spirit that kept going despite the challenges of her environment – a beam of light for those living in darkness." Ruey Loon's opportunity to photograph the war heroine came from another photographer. He remembered Mrs Choy being upbeat and cheerful, very willing to try a few locations and different poses. He recalled scouting the ground floor of the Choy Mackenzie Road home for a tidy background with good lighting that made for a nice composition, one with age and character that told a story about her life.

In the photo you can see a tiny ornament hanging from the light switch. It was a tiny pillow with "A Grandma Is a Very Special Blessing" embroided on it. This detail drew the photographer as it provided an understated subtext to the image.

On 19 July 2006, Mrs Choy had lunch with a 37-year-old Australian traveller introduced by a journalist friend. Over a meal of mulligatawny soup and pan-fried fish, Mrs Choy regaled him with memories of her childhood among the Kadazan, visiting Buckingham Palace thrice, attending the Coronation and becoming tipsy from champagne at the celebration meal afterwards. She made such an impression that her young friend said: "I know she had suffered a lot during the war but she seemed to have the perfect model for living life."

By the end of July, Elizabeth Choy was warded in Tan Tock Seng Hospital. She had felt a numbness in her body – a warning stroke. Although she was discharged after three days, she was admitted to Singapore General Hospital three weeks later where she was discovered to have late-stage pancreatic cancer. She showed no fear when she was told. She was then moved to National University Hospital where Lynette's daughter, Andrea, was training as a medical officer in the Haematology-Oncology Department. Andrea's colleauges kindly arranged for Mrs Choy to be in a room in a quiet corner so she could receive her many visitors.

Mrs Choy informed her family that she did not want treatment. "Mum said she was very prepared and was waiting to go to heaven," Bridget recalls. "She told the doctor: 'Go look after younger patients; no need to spend time on me.'" So she faced death as courageously as she had lived. She refused to be put on drips and hooked to tubes. Unable to stomach food, she drank only juices and soups for two months, losing 15 kg. Still, she combed her hair each day. She put on her glasses before she went to sleep because she wanted to see everything and everyone clearly when she awoke. And many went to visit her. Thus, Mrs Choy spent her final days, as she wished, in her Mackenzie Road home.

Two weeks after she requested to be discharged from hospital, Mrs Choy died peacefully at 2 pm on 14 September 2006, aged 96. She was surrounded by her family who had gathered to pray for her.

President S. R. Nathan, in a tribute, upheld her as a shining example of courage and compassion, saying that she had continued to serve Singapore at an age when most people would have been happy to lead a quiet life of retirement. Prime Minister Lee Hsien

Loong, in turn, said she drove home to young Singaporeans the vital importance of Total Defence like no textbook could.

Mrs Choy's wake was at St Andrew's Cathedral – the first time in the church's history that a wake was allowed to be held there. The honour was given because of Mrs Choy's heroic past.

There she lay, serene in her white coffin wearing the sequined maroon and black cheongsam with an orchid tucked behind her ear. A well-thumbed Bible rested on her chest. From the coffin she faced the spire of the cathedral, the same spire she had spied from her Mackenzie Road home when she first arrived in Singapore in 1929. She had decided then that she would attend the church and used the spire to guide her there. So, through the years, she attended St Andrew's Cathedral, walking ramrod straight up the nave to receive holy communion till she was too ill to do so.

Defence Minister Teo Chee Hean who attended the wake said she is a great inspiration to all Singaporeans, and "will always be a part of our history and our hearts." More than a war heroine, the life of Mrs Choy was distinguished by her grace, dignity, courage, humility and kindness.

The solemn 90-minute funeral service on 16 September was attended by 600 people. Cheryl Ong in her eulogy to her grandmother said her *po po* inspired with her "unconditional love for others and amazing spirit." Tears flowed when the family took a last look at Mrs Choy before the casket was closed. An honour guard from the Girl Guides and Boys Brigade lined the driveway as the hearse left St Andrew's Cathedral for Mandai Crematorium.

The cremation at 4.30 pm was attended by about 100 family members and friends. Afterwards, the life of Elizabeth Choy Su-Moi was celebrated with pink champagne. In proposing the toast, Bridget said: "This is a celebration of Mum's 96 very good years. This is not goodbye. This is till we meet again. Cheers to Mum!"

---

1   Lim Siauw Chong first met Mrs Choy when he was a six-year-old schoolboy at St Andrew's. As an adult, he discovered his former teacher's war experience while doing research.